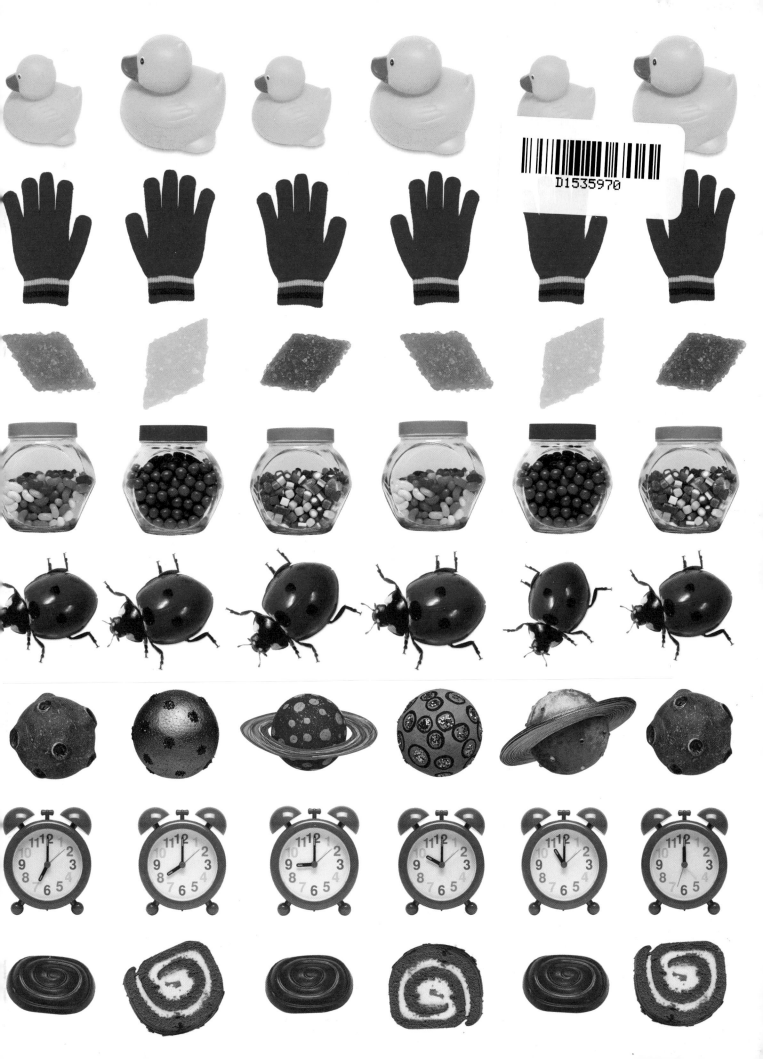

IT'S GREAT TO PLAY AND
FUN TO LEARN

This edition is published by Armadillo
an imprint of Anness Publishing Ltd
Blaby Road, Wigston, Leicestershire LE18 4SE
info@anness.com

www.annesspublishing.com

If you like the images in this book and
would like to investigate using them for
publishing, promotions or advertising, please
visit our website www.practicalpictures.com
for more information.

A CIP catalogue record for this book is available from the British Library.

Publisher Joanna Lorenz
Managing Editor, Children's Books Gilly Cameron Cooper   **Project Editor** Rasha Elsaeed
Editorial Reader Joy Wotton   **Author** Claire Llewellyn   **Photography** John Freeman
Educational Consultants Dr. Naima Browne (*Colours, Counting, Shapes, Sizes, Sums, Time, Words*),
Michael Chinery (*Animals*), Sharon Whittingham (*Science*)
Design and Typesetting Tessa Barwick (*Sizes*), Val Carless (*Counting, Shapes, Time*),
Michael Leaman (*Animals, Colours, Science, Sums, Words*), Louise Millar (*Science*)
Stylists Ken Campbell (*Counting, Science, Shapes, Time*), Marion Eliot (*Counting, Shapes*),
Melanie Williams (*Animals, Science, Sizes, Sums, Time, Words*)

Previously published in nine separate volumes in the Fun To Learn series:
Animals, Colours, Counting, Science, Shapes, Sizes, Sums, Time, and Words

Manufacturer: Anness Publishing Ltd, Blaby Road, Wigston, Leicestershire LE18 4SE, England
For Product Tracking go to: www.annesspublishing.com/tracking
Batch: 6634-22182-1127

PICTURE CREDITS (b=bottom, t=top, c=centre, l=left, r=right)
ABPL:/Anness:Kim Taylor/Warren Photographic:105tl, 105cbr, 107bl, 108c, 109cr, 110cr, 111tl, 112bl, c ,tr, 113tl;/Carol Cavanagh:102br;/ C. Hicks:107cr;
/Lucy Tizard:104cbr, 118bl, 120tr, cr, cl, bl, 121tr;/Robert Pickett:106c;/112tl, cl, bc, 113tl, tr, bl;/Jane Burton 118cl, 120crb;/Kit Houghton:121b;/John Daniels:121cr.
Bruce Coleman Limited:John Shaw:98tl;/Alain Compost:98tr;/Stephen J Krasemann:98bl;/Ingo Arndt:98br;/Jane Burton:99tl;/Gerald Cubitt:99br, 115bl;/Kim Taylor:100tr,
101tl, 105tr, 107br, 113br, 115tr;/Hans Reinhard:100c;/Brian J Coates: 101tr;/Jeff Foott Productions:101br, 102tr;/Dr P Evans:103cr;/Mark Carwardine:103bl;
/Joe McDonald:104t, 119tr;/P. Kaya:105cr;/Charles and Sandra Hood:107cb;/Rod Williams:99tl;/John Cancalosi:110tr;/Alain Compost:110tl;
/Norman Owen Tomalin:110bl;/Christer Fredriksson:110br;/ Michael and Patricia Fogden:111cr;/Mary Plage:111br;/Andy Purcell:112cr;/Dr Frieder Sauer:113cl;/Jorg &
Petra Wegner 119tl;/ Andrew J Purcell:115br;/G Ziesler: 116tr;/Charles & Sandra Hood:117cl;/Pacific Stock: 117cr;/Fritz Prenzel:118br;/Rod Williams:119cl;
/John Cancalosi:119br;/Robert Maier:120cl. FLPA:Michael Gore:99c;/Fritz Polking:99bl, 102bl, 103tr;/ 100br;/David Hosking:102tl, 104b, 105b;
/Ian Cartwright:104cr;/Lee Rue:106tr;/Martin B Withers:108b, 109b, 115cr;/Michel Gunther:109cr, 120br;/John Tinning:113ca;/D Fleetham/ Silvestris:116c, 117br;
/D Perine/Sunset:117t;/W Wisniewski:118tl;/Hugh Clark:118tr;/Brake/Sunset:118cr;/E & D Hosking:119cr;/Mark Newman: 119bl;/Terry Whittaker:106tl, 111tr.
Michael and Patricia Fogden:98c, 100tl, 107tr, 108bl, 109cr, 112br. Natural Science Photos:M W Powles:106b. Oxford Scientific Films:102c;/Steve Turner:115tl.
Papilio Photographic:101cl, 100cr, 100bl, 105c, 108t, 108cr, 116bl, 116br, 117b. Planet Earth Pictures: Peter J Oxford:103cl;/James D Watt:103br;/Mary Clay:109cl;
/Ken Lucas:114tr;/Mark Mattock:114cl;/Edward Coleman:115cl;/Manoj Shah: 123br. The Stock Market:111bl. Zefa Pictures:114bl.

The Publisher would like to thank all the children who modelled in this book.

IT'S GREAT TO PLAY AND
FUN TO LEARN

A stimulating play-and-learn book with over 130 amazing facts, exercises and projects, and more than 5000 bright action-packed photographs

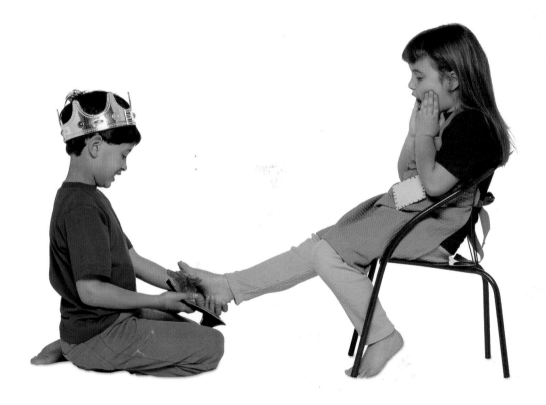

Claire Llewellyn & Arianne Holden

Educational Consultants: Dr. Naima Browne,
Michael Chinery and Sharon Whittingham

ARMADILLO

CONTENTS

Introduction 6

Colours 9

Shapes 37

Words 67

Animals 97

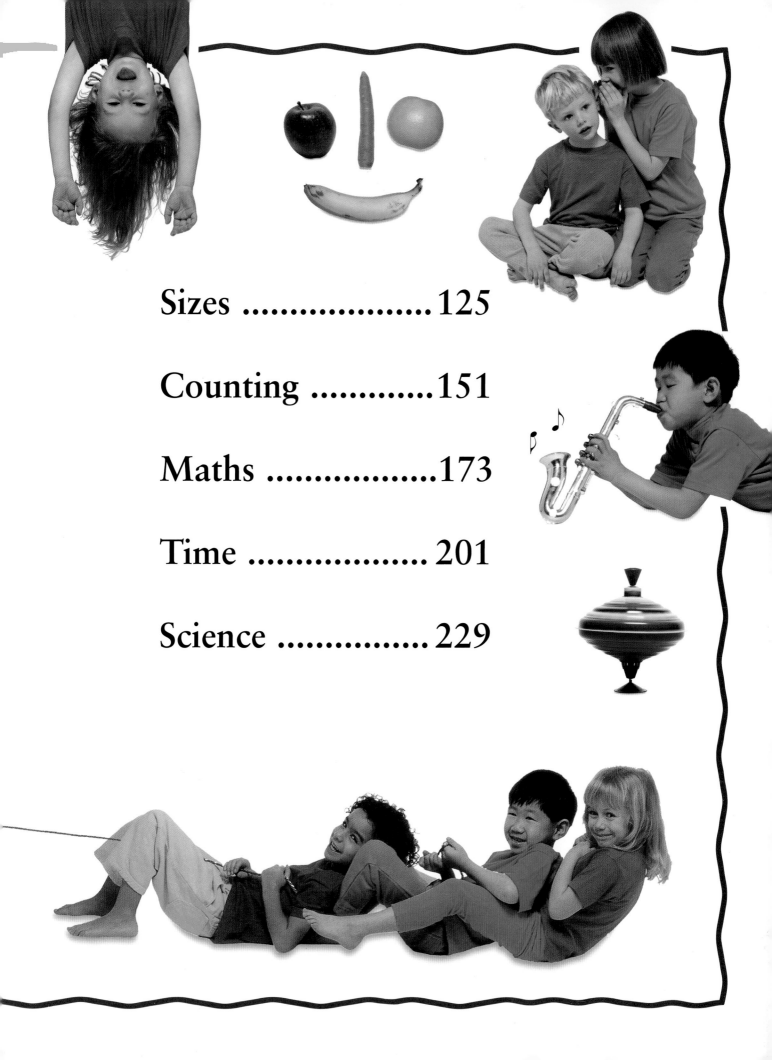

Sizes 125

Counting 151

Maths 173

Time 201

Science 229

INTRODUCTION

Children will discover that it's really fun to learn with this introduction to early learning concepts. The aim is to develop the literacy and numeracy skills that are essential for school. The informative but simple text is complemented by lively, bright photographs, and plenty of fun activities and projects to make. Your child will learn the best way of all – by doing.

Essential skills

This book is arranged thematically in nine sections. Each section practices a set of particular skills. In *Colours* and *Shapes*, children will learn to name and identify the familiar colours, and recognize the properties of different shapes of the objects around them. Concepts such as shades of colour, and mixing and matching colours, are also introduced. *Words* and *Animals* are packed with busy scenes and words that help to build a vocabulary. In *Sizes*, children learn the importance of matching and classifying, and how size is one of the ways in which we group things. *Counting* and *Maths* show how to group things into simple sets, and these sections provide plenty of arithmetic exercises to practice. Time helps children get to grips with halves and quarters, before tackling the idea of minutes and hours. Finally, *Science* introduces children to basic scientific concepts that are part of their everyday lives, such as throwing a ball, pushing a go-cart, and slipping down a slide.

Reading together

Children benefit from adult help when they read a book. Do not expect your child to grasp all the information at once! Your child may respond better when information is repeated several times. Look at one concept at a time, and allow a few days for the information to be absorbed before moving to a new topic.

Talking it through

Try to talk about the things you and your child have found together. Make everyday activities an adventure in learning. Shopping and meal times provide perfect opportunities to talk about food, colour, and shapes, and bath-time is a chance to discuss floating and sinking, and the difference between hot and cold.

Making mistakes

You can check your child's understanding by asking questions: It's cold today, which clothes should you wear? Which animals swim in the sea? At meal times, you could ask – which spoon is the biggest? Which plates are the same size? Encourage your child to answer. Don't worry if the answers are wrong – making mistakes is part of the learning process. The most important thing is that your child has the confidence to answer. Remember to praise all your child's attempts.

Learning by doing

Encourage your child to try the activities. They have been specially created so that they are easy and fun to do. The activities will extend your child's vocabulary and help him or her develop reading and writing skills. They will also help your child understand that it is fun to learn!

Try this!

Make a magic wheel

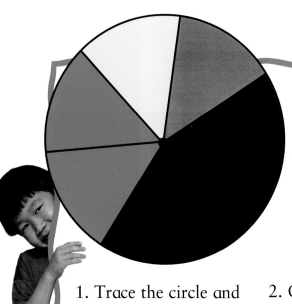

3. Spin the wheel. What colour is it?

1. Trace the circle and lines on to tracing paper. Transfer the tracing to a piece of white card.

2. Cut out the circle. Colour it in exactly as shown. Push a pencil through the middle.

COLOURS

Red

Red is the colour
of ripe tomatoes
and soft, sweet
strawberries.

shades of red

big red hair scrunchies

What will happen
to this tomato?

spicy red
chillies

up ...

up and
down on the
red seesaw

... and down

three scuttling red crabs

Who's going
to eat the
juicy, red
strawberries?

Did you know?

When you're
shy or angry,
your cheeks
can turn
red! Has this
ever happened
to you?

Green

Green is the colour of crisp, crunchy apples and grass.

shades of green

I'm hiding in the long, green grass.

Which green things am I made from?

Hop to it, hoppity green frog!

Green cactus spines are prickly.

oUCH!

Try this!

Cress creature

1. Put damp cotton wool into an egg cup.

2. Scatter cress seeds and water every day.

3. Watch the cress grow.

4. Paint a face on the egg cup. Look at all that green hair!

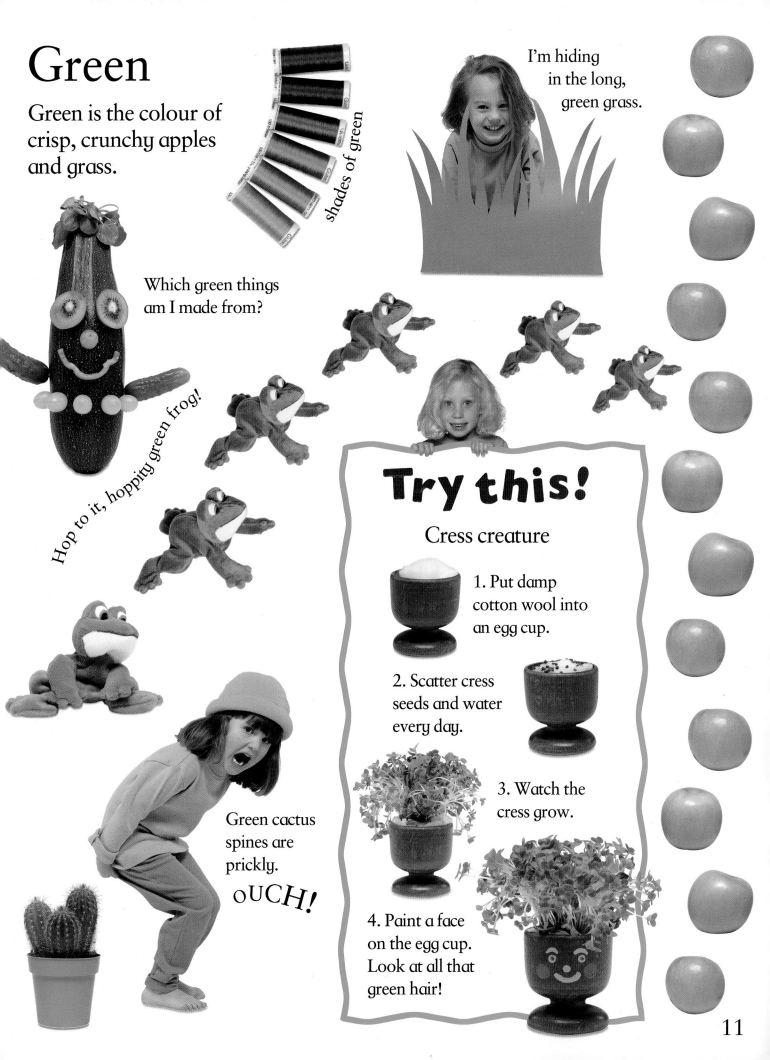

11

Blue

Blue is the colour of the sea and sky on a sunny day. Is the sky blue today?

shades of blue

two blue slithery snakes

Hisss!

A blue cap with blue bobbles.

Ted likes the colour blue.

How many blue whales can you count?

watch out!

three dancing blue aliens

There's a blue frisbee about!

Do you think I can knock down the blue skittles (pins)? Can you play skittles?

Orange

Orange is a happy colour. It is the colour of crunchy carrots and juicy oranges.

shades of orange

Rabbits love carrots.

Try this!

Make frozen orange juice

 1. Wash a small pot.

 2. Trace the top of the pot on to card.

3. Cut it out and make a slit.

 4. Fill the pot with juice and top with the card. Push a stick into the slit and freeze. When frozen, lift off the pot.

orange socks

orange trousers

juicy oranges

orange flowers

Where did I put my orange?

light orange hat and bright orange t-shirt

Do you like eating carrots?

Yellow

Yellow is the colour of sour lemons and sweet bananas.

shades of yellow

How many yellow bananas has this monkey eaten?

quack ...

quack ...

quack ...

bright yellow ducks

a shower of yellow daisies

disco dancing yellow corn on the cob

Try this!

Sunshine cookies

1. In a bowl, mix icing (confectioners') sugar, lemon juice and yellow food dye.

2. Spread icing on to some cookies.

3. Can you taste the lemon? Is it sweet or sour?

14

Purple

Purple is the colour of big, juicy grapes and smooth, shiny plums.

shades of purple

noisy purple shakers

One ...

two ...

... three purple snails.

purple flowers tied with purple ribbon

fluttering purple butterflies

purple recorder

purple grapes

How many aubergines (eggplants) can the chef juggle?

15

Brown

Brown is the colour
of cuddly puppies,
chewy toffee and
muddy footprints.

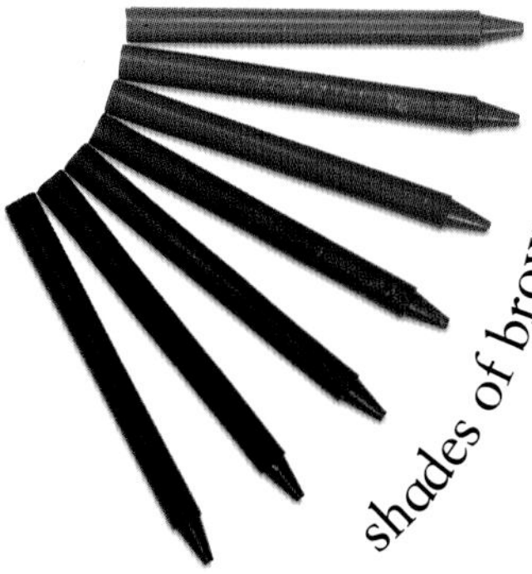

shades of brown

one

two

three
brown
pine
cones

Wombat's
wobbly tower
of brown pine
cones.

a litter of brown puppies

cuddly brown Ted's cartwheeling extravaganza

muddy
brown
footprints

Soft,
brown
feathers feel
ticklish.

chewy
brown toffee
and chocolate

16

Pink

Pink is the colour
of soft, sweet
marshmallows
and your fingernails.

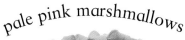

shades of pink

What colour is your tongue?

pale pink marshmallows

 bright pink bowl

rosy pink
bear

Save some
creamy, pink
pudding for me!

Try this!

Making pink dye

1. Put two
beetroots (beets)
in warm water.
Leave till the
water is pink.

2. Remove them.
Place an old white
t-shirt in the water.
Soak overnight.

I'm dressed
in pink from
head to toe.

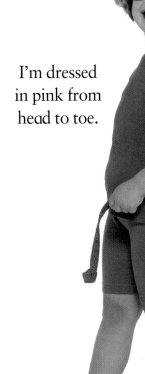

3. Take the t-shirt
out of the bowl.
What colour is it?

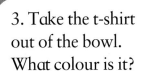

17

Black

You see black when you close your eyes.

What colour are these things?

black bat mask

A juicy black fly for a hungry black spider.

cool black sunglasses

Can you count ten black fingers?

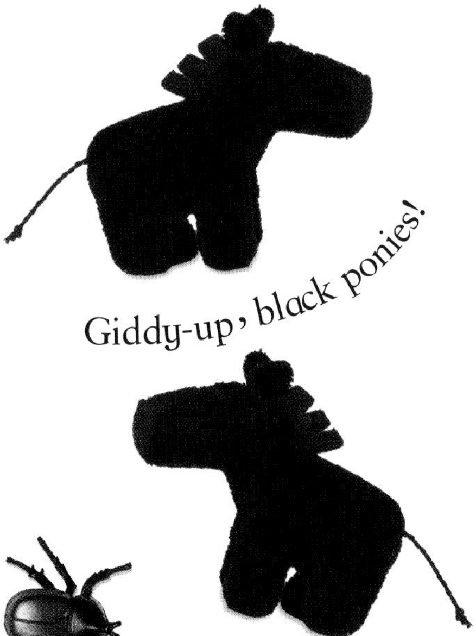

Giddy-up, black ponies!

Where are these shiny black beetles going?

black sheriff's hat

black bowler hat

18

White

White is the colour of snow on a cold winter's day and fluffy clouds on a summer's day.

Can you find any white things?

fluffy white kitten

one

two

three

frisky white lambs

Doctor Rosie will make the polar bear better.

wibbly wobbly snowman

Try this!

Make meringue snow cakes

2. Spoon cream into each meringue.

1. Whisk up some cream in a bowl.

creamy white ice cream.

19

Gold

Gold is a colour that glistens like shining stars and royal crowns.

gold glitter, thread and crayons

glitzy gold wig

three gold rings

two gold bangles

Look at Pirate Ted's sparkling gold treasure.

Try this!

Make a gold crown

1. Draw a crown shape on to card. Cut it out.

2. Glue gold foil on to your crown.

3. Join the ends with adhesive tape.

I'm catching falling stars.

I've won a gold medal!

Silver

Silver is a shiny colour. Sometimes you can see your reflection in things that are silver.

silver crayons, glitter and thread

shiny, silver spaceship

toot!
toot!
toot!

What colour are Ted's weights?

Astronaut Teds wear silver spacesuits and helmets.

brr   brr

silver alarm clock

Look at my silver fancy dress!

ticklish, silver tinsel scarf

Bronze

Bronze is a shiny colour. It looks a little like gold.

bronze thread and crayons

flickering bronze mirror ball

three wild, wiry bronze men

amazing magician in a bronze cloak and hat

abracadabra!

Vroooom!

brilliant bronze racing cars

one

two

three

glowing bronze bows

cool bronze sunglasses

I'm a bronze robot.

dazzling bronze crown

Rainbow

There are seven colours in a rainbow. Do you know what they are called?

red
orange
yellow
green
blue
indigo
violet

Which rainbow colour do you like best?

Ted is painting a rainbow just for you.

stacking rings in rainbow colours

bows of many colours

ruby red

glowing orange

sunshine yellow

cool green

vivid violet

warm indigo

brilliant blue

Dark to light

Colours can be different shades. Some are light shades and some are dark. Can you see the colours getting lighter?

dark blue

Dangling blue ribbons ...

dark red

Ted's red paper hat ...

dark green

A smart green bow tie ...

dark yellow

Pretty yellow petals ...

light blue

... get lighter and lighter and even lighter.

light red

... gets lighter and lighter and even lighter.

light green

... gets lighter and lighter and even lighter.

light yellow

... get lighter and lighter and even lighter.

25

Light to dark

These pictures show some colours getting darker and darker. Run a finger along the lines of colours from light to dark.

light pink

The pink butterflies ...

light brown

The slithery brown snail's shell ...

light purple

The alien's long hair ...

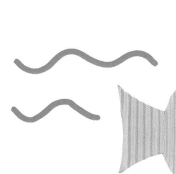

light orange

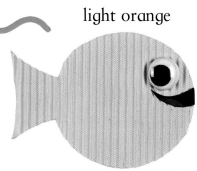

The splishy, splashy fish ...

dark pink

... get darker and darker and darker.

dark brown

... gets darker and darker and even darker.

dark purple

... gets darker and darker and even darker.

dark orange

... get darker and darker and even darker.

27

Mixing colours

When you mix colours, you make new colours. If you have red, blue and yellow paints, you can make all the colours of the rainbow!

red

blue yellow

Blue monster is ready to get mixing!

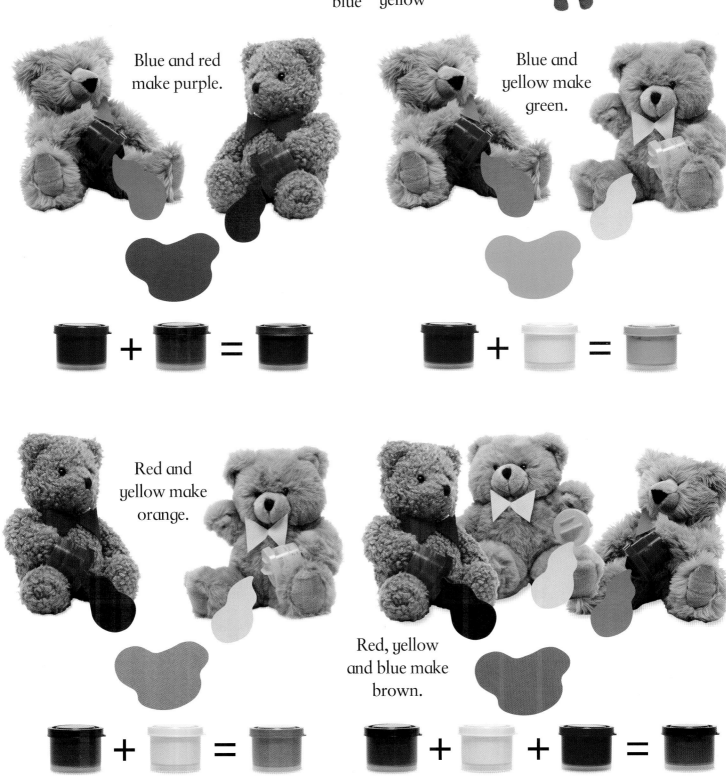

Blue and red make purple.

+ =

Blue and yellow make green.

+ =

Red and yellow make orange.

+ =

Red, yellow and blue make brown.

+ + =

How do you make ...

... orange?

... purple?

... green?

... brown?

Try this!

Mixing colours

1. You will need red, blue and yellow paints, a paintbrush and a container of water.

2. Mix the colours to make brown, green, orange and purple.

3. Use the colours to paint

a brown teddy

a bright green pear

an orange stripy cat

a bunch of purple grapes

29

Making light colours

Make a paint colour lighter by mixing white into it. A light colour is sometimes called a pale colour.

Blue monster loves mixing light colours.

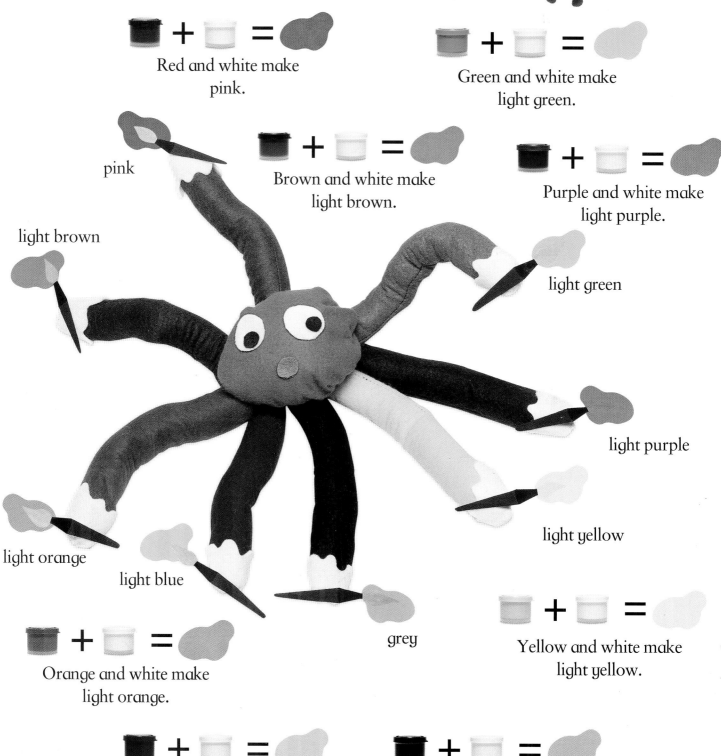

Red and white make pink.

Green and white make light green.

Brown and white make light brown.

Purple and white make light purple.

pink

light brown

light green

light purple

light yellow

light orange

light blue

grey

Orange and white make light orange.

Yellow and white make light yellow.

Blue and white make light blue.

Black and white make grey.

30

Try this!

Making light colours

1. You will need red, yellow, blue and white paint, a paintbrush and a container of water.

2. Choose a colour paint and mix it with white.

3. Make light colours to paint

a grey elephant

a pale blue bird

a pink fluffy bunny

a light green bug

Which light and dark colours can you find at home?

dark pink and light pink shoes

dark purple

light purple

red legs

A light blue t-shirt ...

... and a dark blue t-shirt.

dark red legs

Colours in nature

The natural world is full of wonderful colours. Sometimes things in nature change colour.

Leaves are green in summer, but ...

... gold and brown in autumn (fall).

Grapes can be green or purple.

Young fir cones are green.

Older cones are brown.

Apples can be different colours.

green apple

red apple

red and green apple

Bees collect nectar from colourful flowers.

Sunlight reflects off the golden beetle and dazzles its enemies.

Flamingos are pink when they eat pink shrimps.

Male ducks are colourful. Can you point to the male duck?

The marbled gecko changes the colour of its skin to match its hiding place.

The three-toed sloth is green because a tiny plant grows in its fur. It does not hurt the sloth.

The chameleon is camouflaged to match the branch.

33

Treasure hunt

Choose red, green, blue or yellow. Then find, make or draw all the things pictured along the matching coloured line. You can play this alone or with friends.

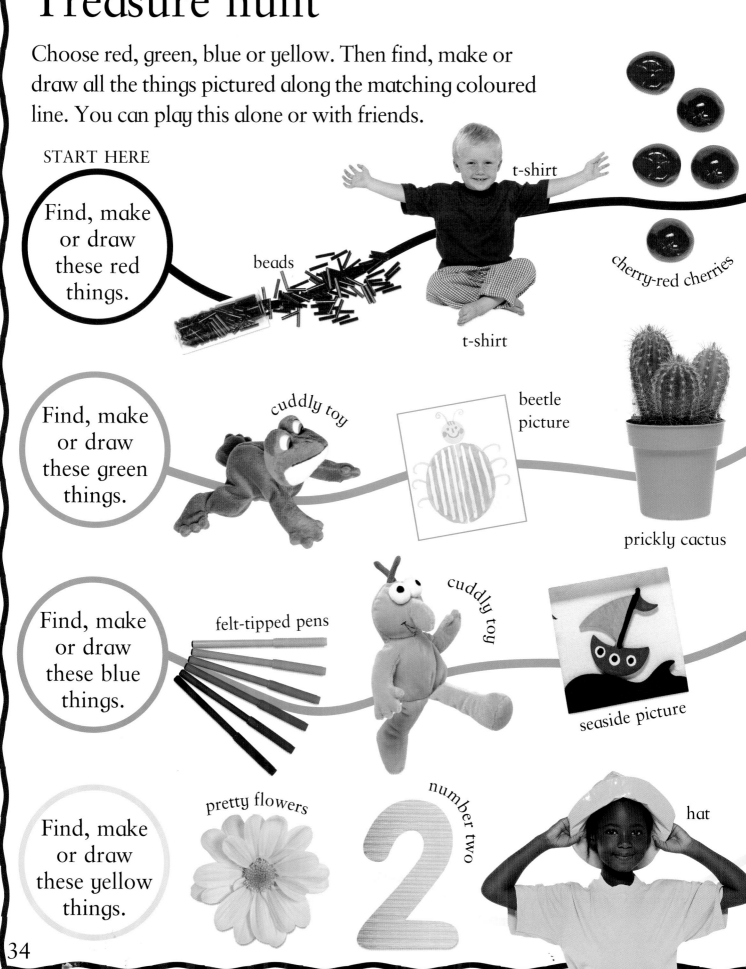

START HERE

Find, make or draw these red things.

beads

t-shirt

t-shirt

cherry-red cherries

Find, make or draw these green things.

cuddly toy

beetle picture

prickly cactus

Find, make or draw these blue things.

felt-tipped pens

cuddly toy

seaside picture

Find, make or draw these yellow things.

pretty flowers

number two

hat

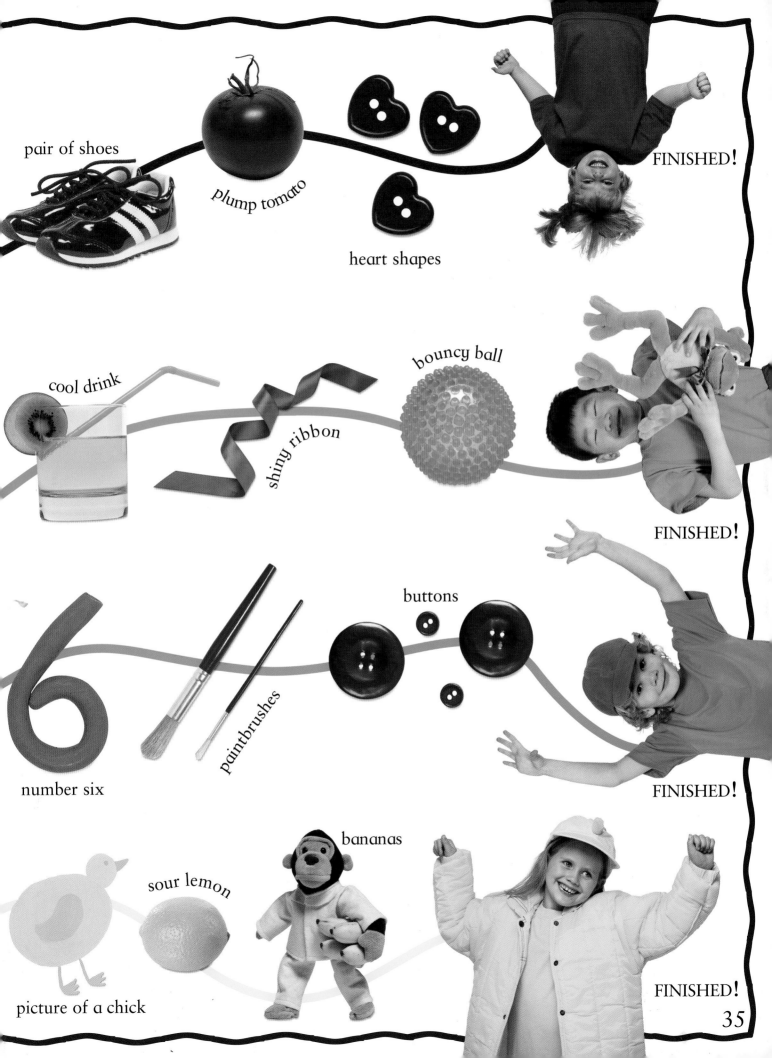

pair of shoes

plump tomato

heart shapes

FINISHED!

cool drink

bouncy ball

shiny ribbon

FINISHED!

number six

paintbrushes

buttons

FINISHED!

picture of a chick

sour lemon

bananas

FINISHED!

35

Try this!

Fingerprinting

1. Colour a fingertip with a felt-tipped pen.

2. Press it on to a piece of paper.

3. Look closely to see the wiggly lines.

SHAPES

Square

This is a square. It has four straight sides, which are exactly the same length, and four matching corners.

square

You need four people to make a square. They need to be the same size.

Can you count all the squares on my shirt...

...on my trousers (pants)...

...and on my shoes?

Try this!

Patchwork picture

1. Cut out lots of small paper squares from old magazines.

2. Fit the squares together to make a picture.

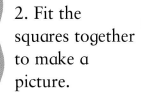

3. Stick your picture squares on to a piece of paper.

I like painting bright red squares.

Can you find two squares in this picture?

square, blue picture frame

Look at this jolly clown picture in a square frame.

How many squares can you see?

Do you know which games are played on these squares?

Can you see the squares on Teddy's ribbon?

Can you play noughts and crosses (tic-tac-toe)?

This teddy has squares on his scarf

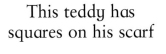

Do any of your clothes have squares on them?

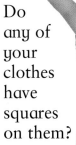

Here is a square envelope...

...for a square card.

Mr H Nelson
43 Victory Road
Portsmouth

Squares fit together without leaving a gap. This is called tessellating.

39

Triangle

A triangle has three straight sides and three corners.

triangles

Sometimes, a triangle has three matching sides and three matching corners.

yummy, chocolate triangles

Three people can make a triangle.

Look at these stripy triangles!

What shape is this slice of pizza?

Do you know what this instrument is called?

Try this!

Make a string of flags

1. Cut large triangles out of paper.

2. Stick them to a piece of string.

3. Hang the string of flags in your room.

triangular presents

Look at Teddy's triangular hat!

Look at all these triangles. Do any of them have matching sides?

colourful, triangular sails

Can you see any triangles here? How many can you count?

How many triangles are there on this crown?

yellow and blue triangular flag

Triangles will fit together without leaving a space.

41

Circle

A circle is a round shape with no straight sides.

circle

A circle will spin…

A circle does not have any corners.

yummy, circular cookies

How many circles can you see?

...and a circle will roll.

circular wheels on a toy train

Try this!

Make the wheels go round

1. Draw and cut out a car shape on card.

2. Draw and cut out two circles.

3. Draw and cut out two squares.

4. Attach the wheels to the car with paper clips. Which wheels turn the best?

Where are the circles on this bike?

You can make patterns with circles.

You can make circles with...

wobbly, round eyes

...your fingers...

...your arms and...

...your mouth!

43

Oblong

An oblong has four straight sides.
It looks like a stretched square.

oblong

An oblong has…

…four matching corners.

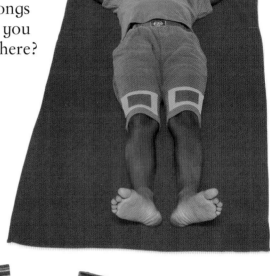

How many
oblongs
can you
see here?

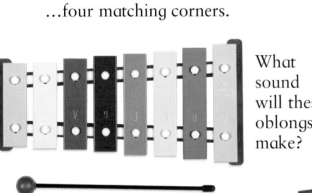

What
sound
will these
oblongs
make?

oblongs
on socks

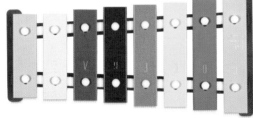

tasty,
chocolate
oblongs

blue and
pink
oblong
flag

Do you have an
oblong mirror?

a string of oblong birthday cards

oblong, animal dominoes

Do you use...

...an oblong pencil case...

...an oblong ruler...

...or an oblong calculator at school?

Try this!

Edible oblongs

1. Ask an adult to make you a slice of toast.

2. Cut the toast into fingers.

3. Dip the oblong fingers in a boiled egg and eat – it is delicious!

How many oblongs are there in this tower?

ZOO

Look at the oblong sign. Where is it pointing?

Oblongs fit together without leaving a space.

45

Spiral

A spiral is a smooth, coiled shape without any corners.

spiral

swirly, spiral seashell

spirally skipping rope

sticky, spiral candies

spiral spring...

...BOING!

slithery, spirally snails

Follow the spiral shoelace trail.

Can you see the spirals in the pen?

You can drink through this spiral.

spiral china cat

46

spirally hair

Teddy's T-shirt has a wiggly pink spiral on it!

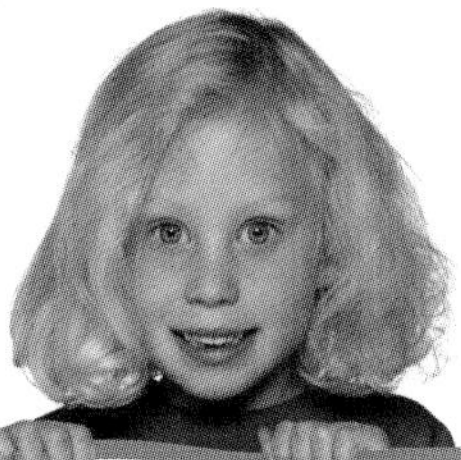

Try this!

Make a spiral pot

1. Roll some dough into a long, thin sausage shape.

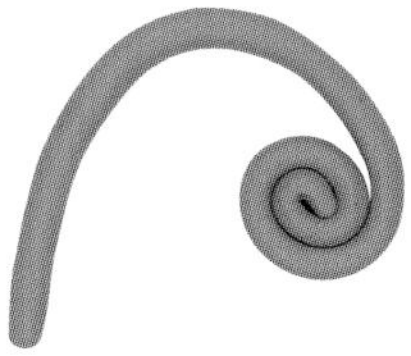

2. Curl your dough round in a spiral.

3. Build up the sides by winding the dough round.

Look at the spirals on the spinning top!

Can you paint a spiral?

What is this spiral made from?

You can make patterns with spirals.

47

Diamond

A diamond has four matching, straight sides. How is it different from a square?

diamond

diamond trellis

flyaway, diamond kites

diamond playing cards

Look at all the diamonds on my suit!

Did you know?

You can make a diamond out of two triangles.

noisy, diamond drum

Diamonds fit together without leaving a space.

48

Semicircle

A semicircle is half a circle. It has one curved side and one straight side.

semicircle

You can make a semicircle!

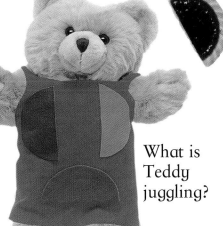

What is Teddy juggling?

Sometimes, the Sun looks like a semicircle.

What is this semicircle called?

Can you paint a sunrise?

Can you see the bird on this semicircular hook?

Did you know?

You can make a circle out of two semicircles.

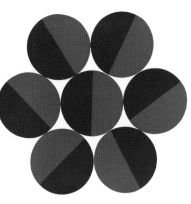

Semicircles will fit together, but the circles leave gaps.

49

Heart

A heart is a curved shape with a dip in the top. Hearts make people think of love.

Teddies LO♥E hearts

shiny, heart balloons

heart

Who would you give this cake to?

heart-shaped chocolates

Can you see the heart I am wearing?

Try this!

Make a love heart

1. Fold a big piece of red paper in half. Draw half a heart on it.

2. Cut it out, then open it out and you have a heart.

3. Draw all the things you love.

4. Stick them on your love heart.

Hearts will fit together, but they leave spaces in-between.

Star

A star has several straight sides that join together to make points.

star

glittery, golden star

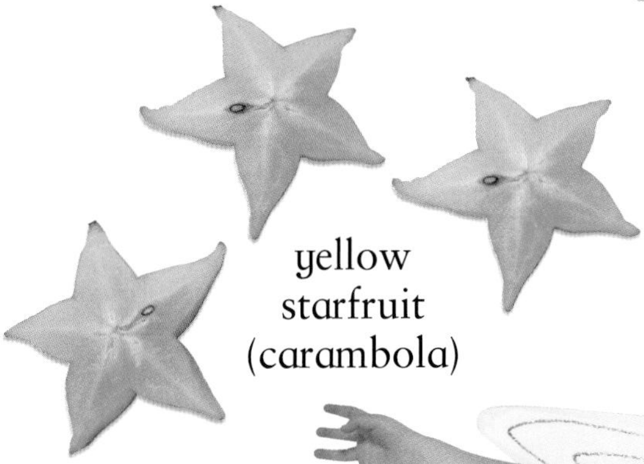

yellow starfruit (carambola)

What do you think the frog will turn into?

Did you know?

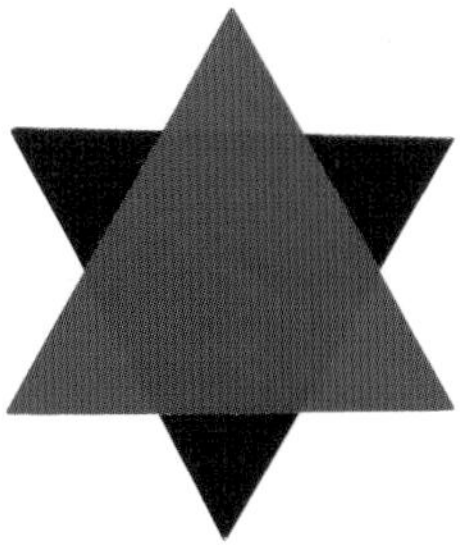

You can make a star out of two triangles.

funny, starry sunglasses

star-shaped candles

Stars fit together, but they leave spaces in-between.

51

Cube

A cube is a solid shape with six matching, square sides.

cube

tumbling cube dice

Do you think there is anything inside the three pretty cube boxes?

Can you count how many fun cubes this smiling juggler is juggling?

Try this!

Cubes on sticks

1. Cut some cheese and pineapple cubes.

2. Thread a cube of cheese on to a cocktail stick. Then add a pineapple cube.

3. Thread one more cheese cube for a tasty treat!

brilliant building blocks

52

What shape is this crane hoisting up?

Sometimes, candles are cubes. What other shapes can you see on the candle?

Do you like giving presents?

crunchy, brown sugar cubes

Teddy is building a tower of cubes.

What shape is this present?

What is inside the box?

Peepo!

53

Cuboid

A cuboid is a solid shape with six flat sides.

cuboid

big, blue
cuboid truck

Cuboid boxes
sometimes have
toys inside!

Try this!

Cuboid picture box

1. Ask an adult to copy the shape of a cuboid box on to paper.

2. Draw six different pictures on to the paper. Colour them in.

3. Stick the pictures on to the box.

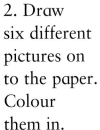

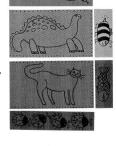

What shape is the ice in this glass?

cold, chocolate ice-cream cuboid

Who is hiding in this cuboid?

Do you like cookies? What other cuboids can you eat?

exciting, cuboid cooker

Teddy is too big for my cuboid suitcase!

shiny, tough, cuboid CD case

smooth, creamy, cuboid dessert

Tuneful Teddy is playing a cuboid harmonica.

What shape are the building bricks?

Would you like to eat a chocolate from my cuboid box?

Cylinder

A cylinder is a solid shape. It has a circle at each end and one smooth curved face.

cylinder

These cylinders have...

...cylindrical sequins inside!

Tins can be cylinders.

You can play with cylinders!

a tall tower of cylinders

How many cylinders can you see here?

What would you do with these cylinders?

You can save money in this cylinder!

cylinders full of sparkly glitter

cylindrical rolls of party paper

What shape is the telescope?

Sometimes, you can crawl through cylinders.

Try this!

Cylinder stamps

1. Ask an adult for the cork from a wine bottle.

2. Paint a face on one end.

3. Stamp the cork on a piece of paper.

What sound does this cylinder make?

noisy, tooting cylinders

Pyramid

A pyramid is a solid shape, with four triangular faces.

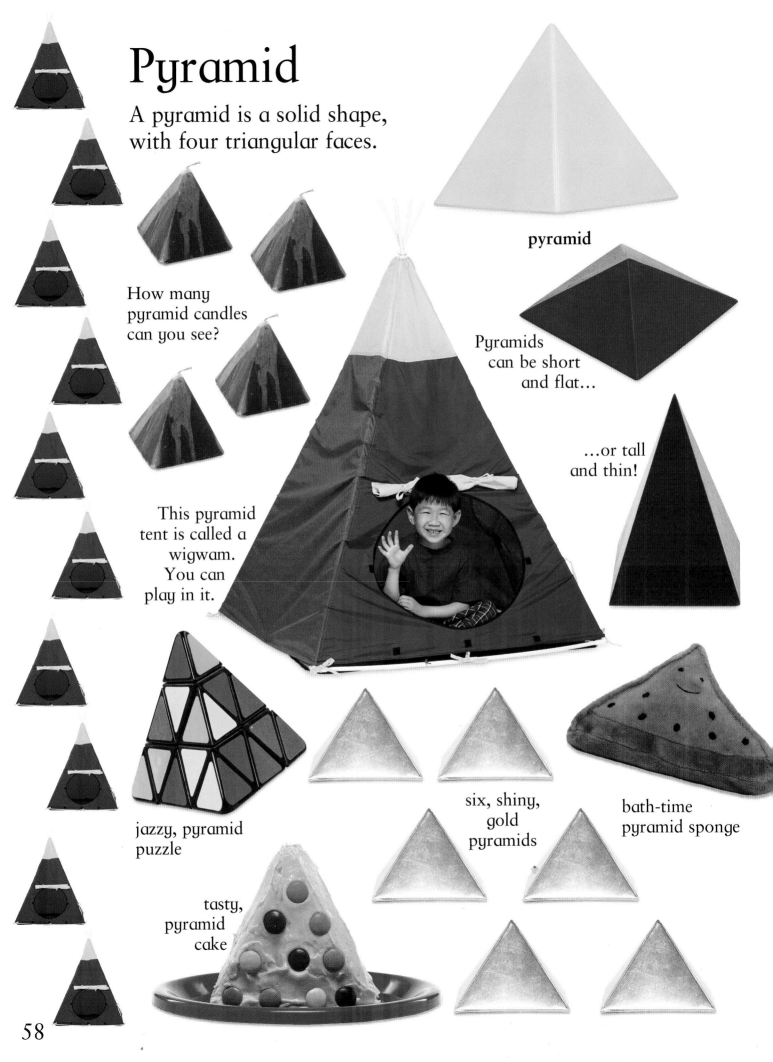

pyramid

How many pyramid candles can you see?

Pyramids can be short and flat...

...or tall and thin!

This pyramid tent is called a wigwam. You can play in it.

jazzy, pyramid puzzle

six, shiny, gold pyramids

bath-time pyramid sponge

tasty, pyramid cake

58

A cone is a solid shape with a pointed end, and one curved face.

cone

funny party hats

What's inside this cone?

Cones are perfect for holding ice creams…

….or candies!

Peepo!

Try this!

Coneheads

1. Draw a big circle on a big piece of thin card.

2. Cut it out. Cut in from the edge to the middle.

3. Slide one edge under the other to make a cone. When it fits your head, stick it together with glue.

happy clown in a cone hat

A big cone like this can make your voice sound LOUDER.

59

Sphere

A sphere is a round solid shape, with no edges or corners.

Look at this enormous sphere. Would you like to play with it?

sphere

What shape are the bubbles?

Can you balance a sphere on your head?

These spheres have funny faces.

Pom-poms are spheres.

Look at our hair bobbles!

What shape is this pumpkin?

Look at me! I'm bobbing for apples.

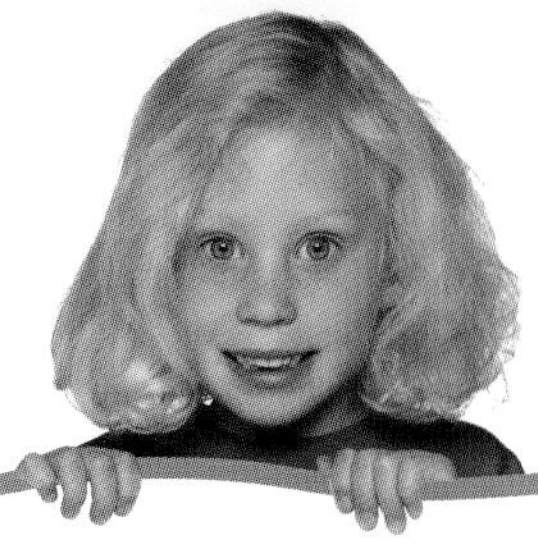

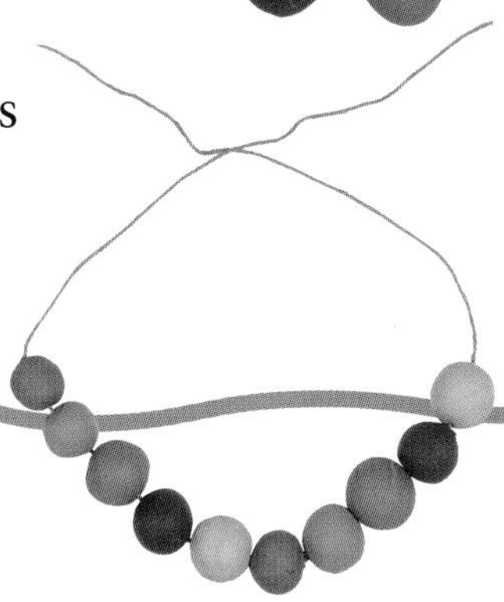

crunchy, spherical apples

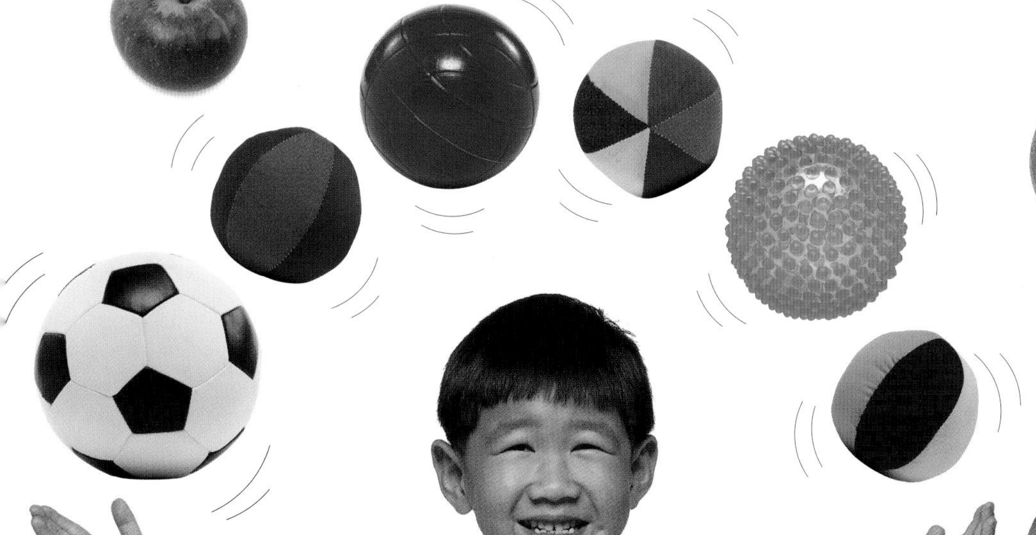

Try this!
Make a spherical necklace

1. Roll some dough into spheres. Make a hole in the middle of them.

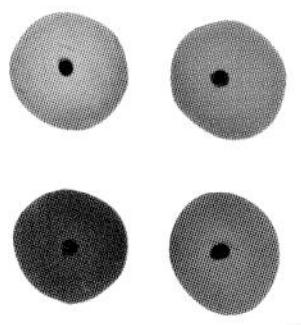

2. Thread your spheres on to a piece of cord. Now you can wear your spheres.

juicy, spherical oranges

Quick, Jake! Catch the ball before it rolls away.

Spheres are great for juggling! Can you juggle?

, in nature

everywhere.
...nd you and
shapes
...see.

Can you see the heart shape on the snake's skin?

What shape are these tomatoes?

When you cut a watermelon in half you can see a circle.

shiny, red, spherical berries

round, shiny apples

What shape are the kitten's ears?

Ferns have tightly curled spiral leaves.

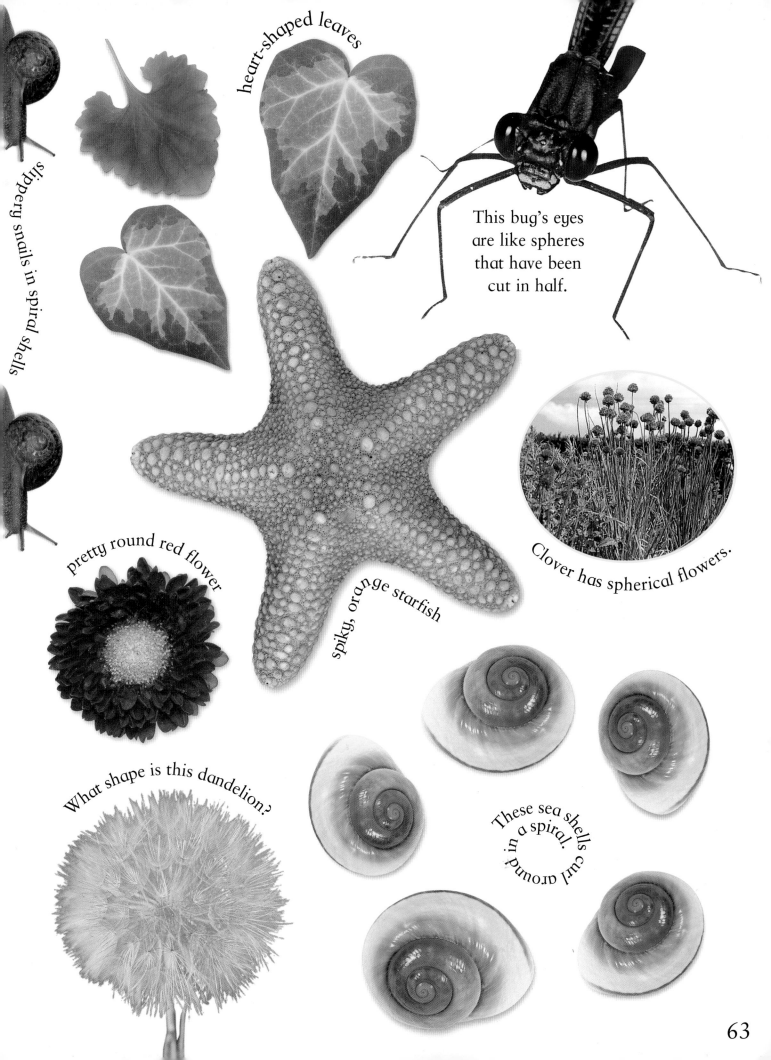

slippery snails in spiral shells

heart-shaped leaves

This bug's eyes are like spheres that have been cut in half.

Clover has spherical flowers.

pretty round red flower

spiky, orange starfish

What shape is this dandelion?

These sea shells curl around in a spiral!

63

Shapes race

The snails, Wiggly William and Curly Kate, are going to see the semicircle juggler. Roll a die and move your marker to see who will get there first.

markers or buttons

die

Wiggly William

Curly Kate

START

1

2

3

4 Overtake the Square Bears. Move on to the next yellow square.

5

6

7 Stop to listen to Triangle Ted. Miss a turn.

8

9

10 Meet the Heart Bears. Move on to the next heart.

11

64

15

16

17

The diamond clown is very lucky. Have another turn.

14

13

12

18

19

20

Find a cube present. Go forward 2 spaces.

21

22

23

24

25

You have reached the semicircle juggler. How many semicircles can you see?

FINISH

1. Find 7 things that feel very different. Put them in a bag.

rough bark

feather

sticky lollipop

bath sponge

jam tart

metal dish

cuddly toy

Try this!

Touchy feely game

2. Ask a friend to feel what is inside the bag. Can they name the things without peeking?

WORDS

Getting up, getting ready

Waking up

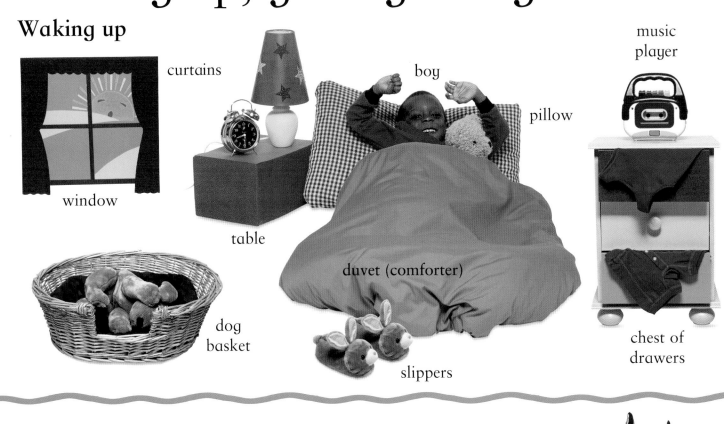

curtains

music player

boy

pillow

window

table

duvet (comforter)

dog basket

chest of drawers

slippers

Getting dressed

jester's hat

baby suit

shirt

t-shirt

cardigan

dress

socks

trousers (pants)

jumpsuit

bootees

shoes

alarm clock

lamp

hairbrush

slippers

clothes hanger

sponge

rubber duck

In the bathroom

mirror

toothpaste

diving ted

shelf

wind-up toy

bathtub

sponge

Hair fun

ribbon

hair gel

scrunchies

headband

Ready to go

rain hat

umbrella

sun hat

knitted hat

summer dress

coat

raincoat

toy dog

rubber boots

sandals

snow

soap

toothbrush

scarf

comb

gloves

Playgroup

Puppet show

stage

popcorn

audience

cushion

Water playtime

shells

play pots

watering can

Drawing

backpack

pencils

pencil pot

paper

felt-tipped pens

Snack time

bookshelves

books

cookies

milk

Did you know?

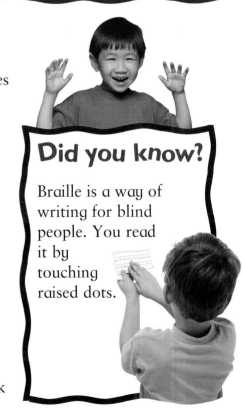

Braille is a way of writing for blind people. You read it by touching raised dots.

puppet

pencil

adhesive tape

pencil sharpener

eraser

tug boat

Cleaning up

duster

ironing board

laundry

washing basket

dustpan

cuddly toys

Try this!

Make a poster

1. Cut out a square of coloured paper. Stick a white label on it.

2. Write on it the name of your playgroup. Draw some of the friends you see there.

Fun Group

Painting

easel

apron

paint pots

green paint

Cutting and pasting

glitter

glue stick

picture

paper shapes

scissors

 dustpan

 brush

 triangle

 square

 circle

blue paint

Shopping

Writing a shopping list

shopping list

shopping basket

jar

Try this!

Write a shopping list

Do you need anything from the supermarket? Write a list of the food you want to buy. Draw the food next to the word.

bread

ketchup

apples

soup

grapes

At the supermarket

washing powder

canned vegetables

fruit juice

cereal

shopping trolley

bread

bread basket

glass jars

jelly beans

candies

bananas

chocolates

strawberry

paper bag

till

72

Buying fruit and vegetables

Bananas

sign

Apples

tomato

pears

juggling Ted

apples

onions

cauliflowers

bananas

potatoes

Paying at the till

store assistant

customer

Supermarket

box

receipt

paper bag

plum

shopping basket

toilet roll

carrot

shopping trolley

purse

Cooks at work

casserole
dish

pan

handle

cup

jug
(pitcher)

cup

containers

eggs

chef's
hat

apron

Getting ready to cook

cookbooks

dial   stove   timer

oven

oven
door

cooker

Icing cupcakes

food dye

paper cases

cake
decorations

bag

cupcakes

Try this!

Cake icing (frosting)

1. Pour 115g/4oz/1 cup of icing (confectioners') sugar into a bowl.

2. Add 120ml/4fl oz/ ½ cup of water to the sugar. Stir them together.

3. Mix in 5ml/1 tsp of red food dye. Now spread the mixture on to some cakes.

mixing
bowl   whisk

frying pan

wooden
spoons

casserole dish

Making pancakes

pancake

chocolate syrup

cream

honey

chef

table leg

Table setting

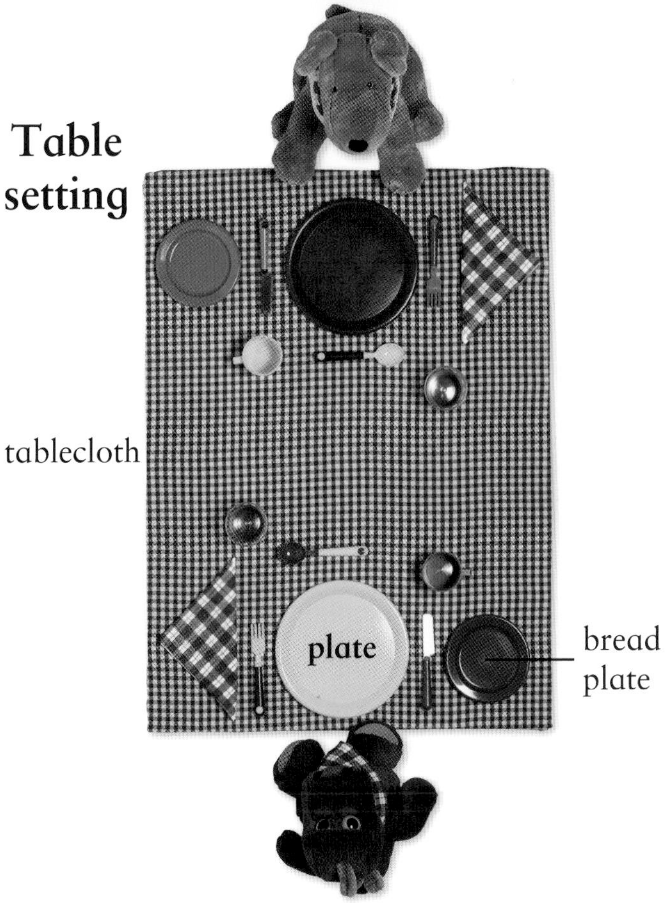

tablecloth

plate

bread plate

Washing dishes

dishwashing liquid

scourers

duster

gloves

bowl

Cleaning up

garbage container

cleaner

broom

soap suds

bucket

mop

napkin

scales

fork

knife

lemon

plate

spoon

brush

75

Playtime

Toy farm

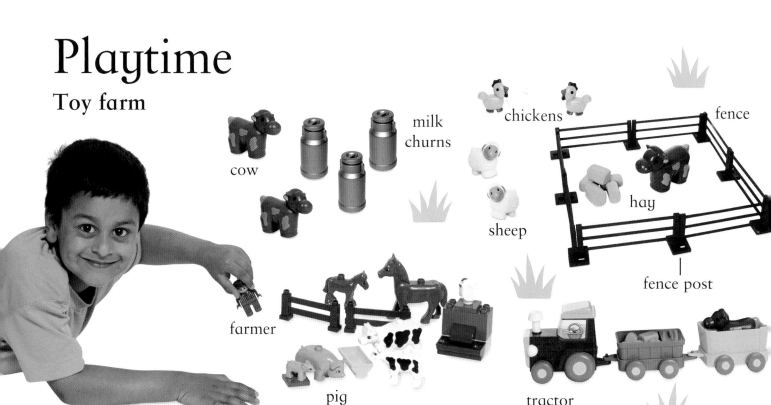

cow

milk churns

chickens

fence

sheep

hay

fence post

farmer

pig

tractor

Trucks

crane

garbage truck

blocks

dump truck

Try this!

Play I Spy

Choose an object you can see in the room. Tell your friends which letter the word begins with. Can they guess what it is? Whoever guesses correctly is the next to choose.

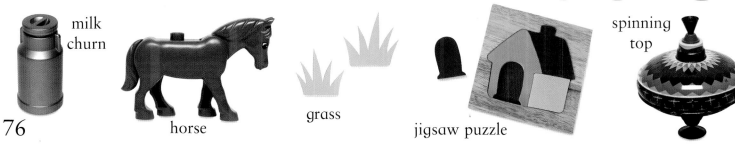

milk churn

horse

grass

jigsaw puzzle

spinning top

Outside

toy
mouse

seesaw

toy
elephant

tunnel

slide

steps

rocker

hopper

pond

Toys

ball

toy bag

racing car

marbles

Train set

signal

station
master

station

funnel

carriage

steam
train

train
track

cement
mixer

ball

flower

Jack-in-
the-box

77

A good story

Fairy

wings

magic
wand

stars

mice

pumpkin

Witch

cobweb

broomstick

spider

potion
bottles

slime

snail

snail trail

King

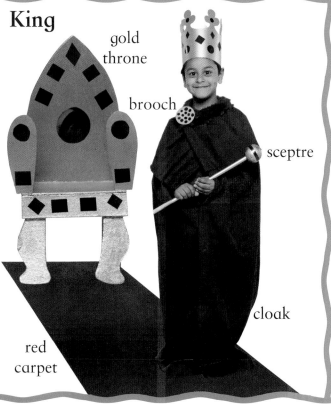

gold
throne

brooch

sceptre

cloak

red
carpet

Cowboy

saddle

belt

lasso

rocking horse

tassel

cowboy
boots

cactus

magic
wand

crown

tiara

sceptre

cauldron

Pirates

parrot

pirate hat

map

treasure chest

spyglass

North American Indians

sticks

tepee

Try this!

Write a potion recipe

1. What would you put in a potion? Think up a gruesome recipe. Then find a large piece of paper.

2. Draw pictures of your gruesome ingredients. Write the name of each one beside it.

slime

bat juice

spider

mouse

feather

flames

camp fire

cowboy hat

gold necklace

spyglass

eye patch

earring

feather headdress

Moving along

Driving to the petrol (gas) station

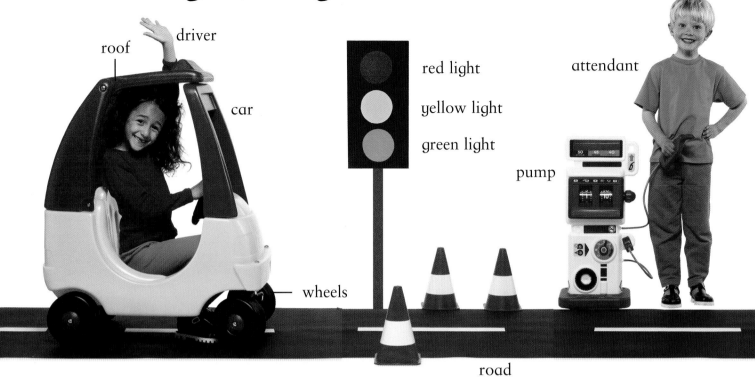

roof

driver

car

wheels

red light

yellow light

green light

attendant

pump

road

Cycling

brake

handlebars

seat

tricycle

bicycle

pedal

spokes

stabilizer

Skateboarding

kneepad

skateboard

wheel

steering wheel

traffic cone

elbow pads

helmet

traffic light

Flying

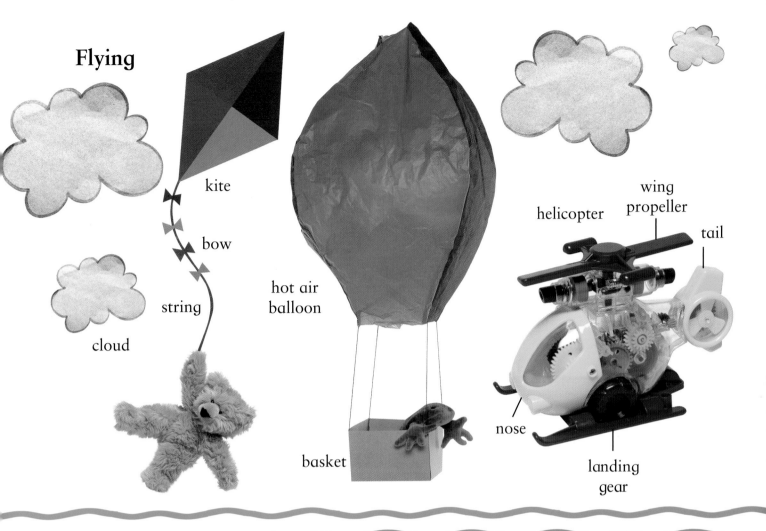

cloud

kite

bow

string

hot air
balloon

basket

helicopter

wing
propeller

tail

nose

landing
gear

Sailing

sailor

sail

waves

flag

Try this!

Bus trip

me Jan Paul Lucy Ted

1. Draw a picture of a bus that
you would like to travel on.
Invite some friends to join you.

2. Draw your friends in
their seats. Then, write
their names above them.

hose

cloud

boat

safety ring

81

Jobs for fun

Doctor

stethoscope

lab coat

patient

first aid kit

Carpenter

hard hat

tool shelf

spanner (wrench)

pliers

overalls

tool box

photographer

Clown

wig

pom-pom

water squirter

Movie star

headband

feather boa

bracelets

dress

flowers

microphone

reporter

notepad

thermometer

telephone

bandage

plasters (Band-Aids)

bolts

82

Office worker

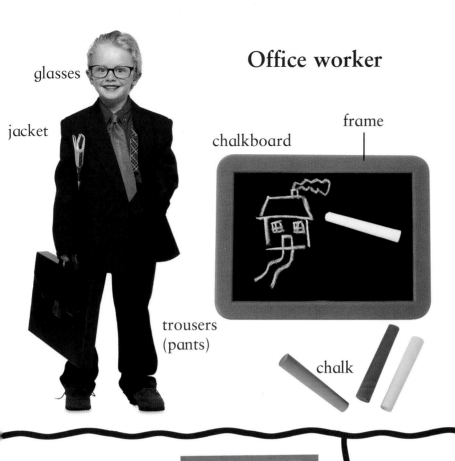

glasses

jacket

trousers
(pants)

chalkboard

frame

chalk

Try this!

Dream job

I'm a clown!
I work in a circus.

Think of the job
you'd most
like to do. Draw a
picture of the outfit
you would wear
for your job.
Draw a speech
bubble and then write
in it who you are.

Detective

Wanted

wanted
poster

hat

magnifying
glass

pawprint

office
desk

chair

Astronaut

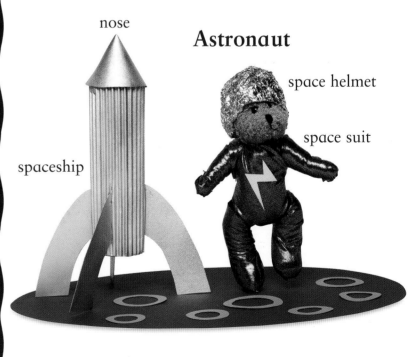

nose

space helmet

space suit

spaceship

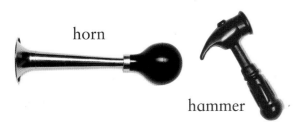

horn

hammer

briefcase

tie

camera

83

Making music

Jazz band

mouthpiece

saxophone

bugle

trumpet

Ted rock band

drum

drummer

notes

guitarist

guitar

Percussion music

castanets

lead singer

Choir

ruffle collar

singer

song sheet

Did you know?

Music is written in notes, not words. The names of the notes are A, B, C, D, E, F and G.

compact disc case

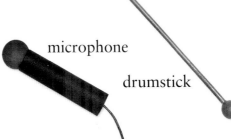

headphones

microphone

drumstick

sheet music

baton

Hula dancer

maraca

grass skirt

ankle garland

Listening to music

headphones

radio

music player

compact discs

Orchestra

musicians

scratcher

conductor

baton

harmonica

triangle

xylophone

maraca

loudspeaker

neck garland

tambourine

Party time

Decorating

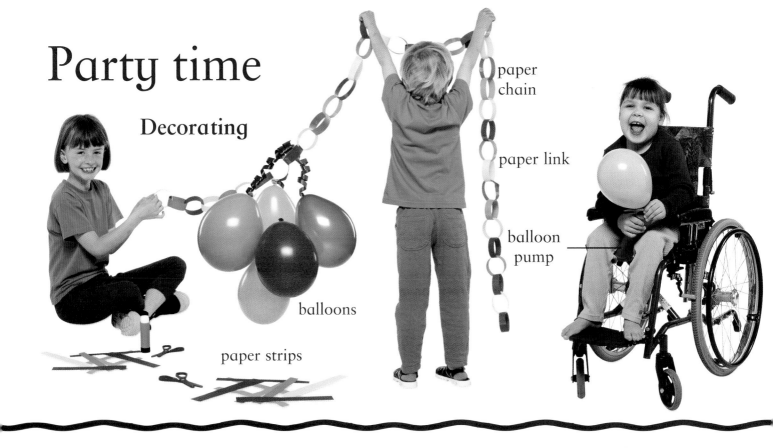

paper chain

paper link

balloon pump

balloons

paper strips

Piles of presents

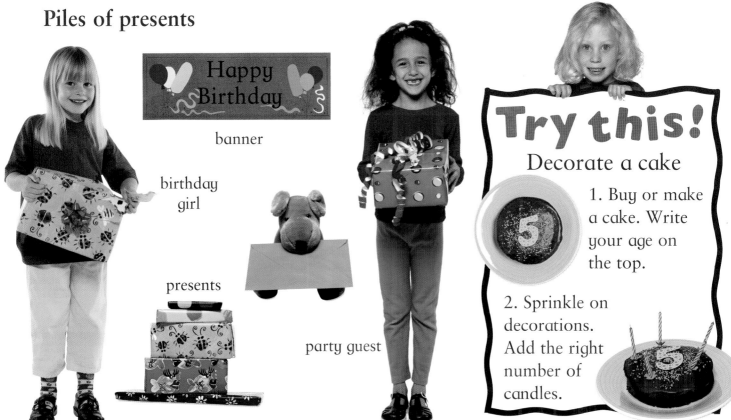

Happy Birthday

banner

birthday girl

presents

party guest

Try this!

Decorate a cake

1. Buy or make a cake. Write your age on the top.

2. Sprinkle on decorations. Add the right number of candles.

birthday card

 balloon pump

 bow

 tarts

party hat

Party treats

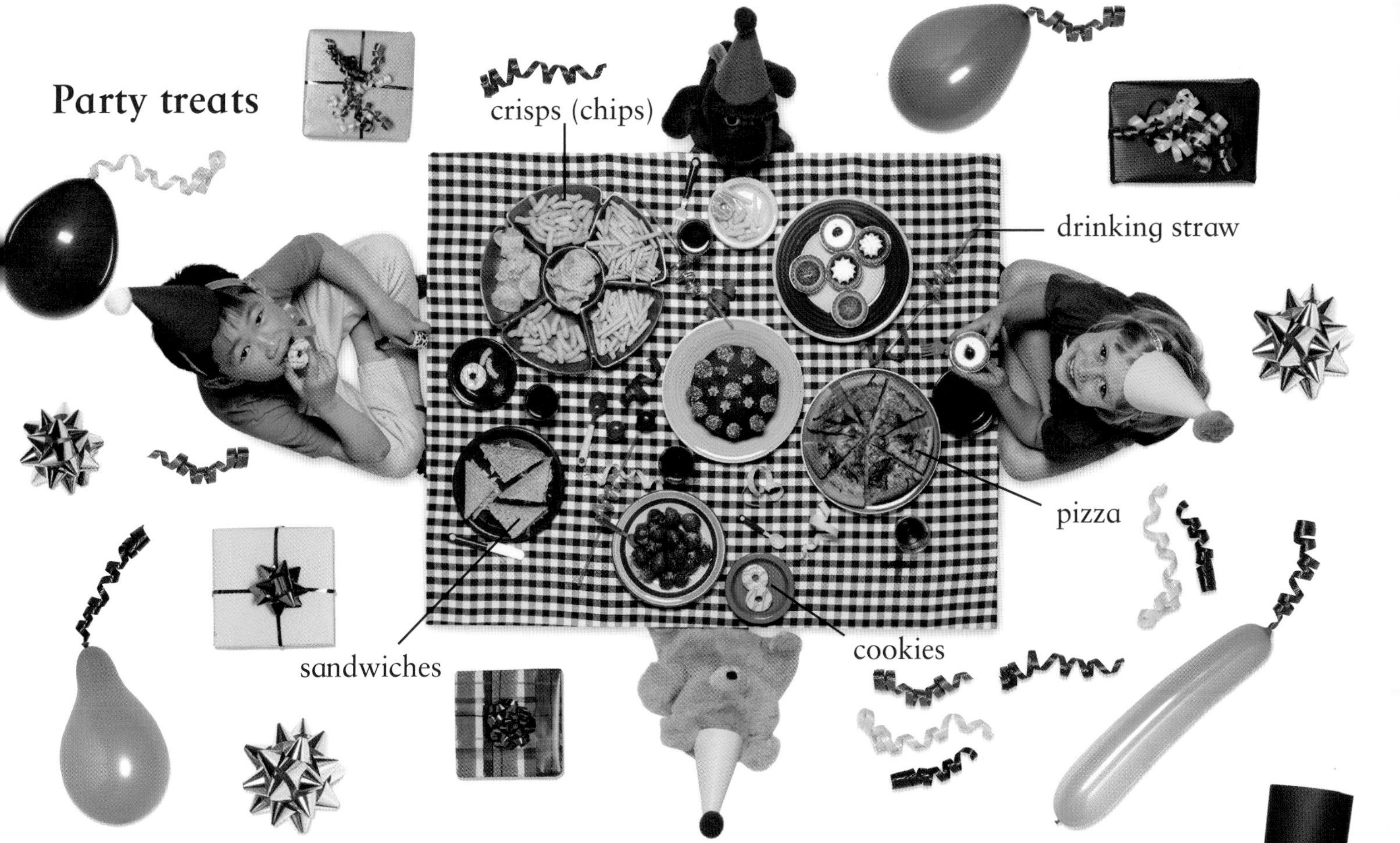

crisps (chips)

drinking straw

pizza

sandwiches

cookies

Magic show

audience

plate
spinner

acrobat

magician

cape

trick
box

magic
wand

birthday
cake

top hat

ribbon

candle

87

Sunny seaside

At the beach

sun

sun umbrella

sunbather

surfboard

beach bag

towel

Fishing

baseball cap

fishing net

Did you know?

Sometimes symbols are used instead of words.

This sign means that there is water ahead.

This sign means that children cross here.

shells

pincers

rock pool

sand

shell

sunglasses

sun hat

swimsuit

crab

Ready for a swim

snorkel

swimmer

swimming hat

armband

inflatable raft

sponge

starfish

Refreshments

Ice Cream

ice cream sign

ice lolly (popsicle)

ice cream

sandcastle

sand shapes

Playing

sun hat

beach ball

bucket

turret

sandals

spade (shovel)

ice cube tray

flippers

goggles

ring

sunscreen

Sport crazy

Soccer

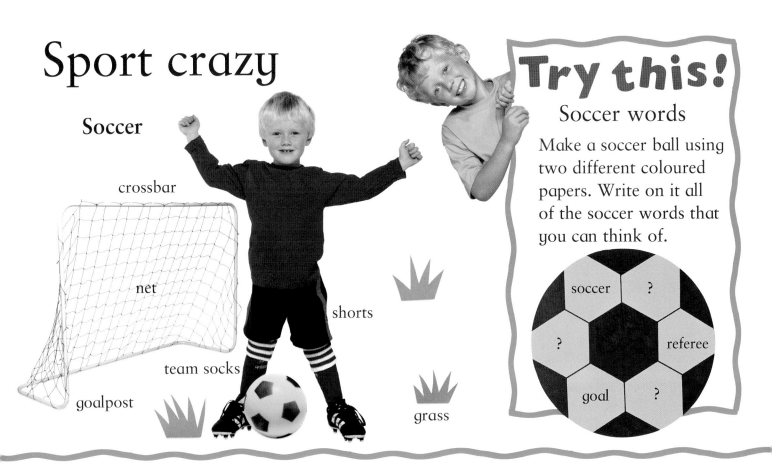

crossbar

net

shorts

team socks

goalpost

grass

Try this!

Soccer words

Make a soccer ball using two different coloured papers. Write on it all of the soccer words that you can think of.

soccer ? ? referee goal ?

Sports day

runners

hopper

skipper

referee

sack

jump rope

starting line

soccer ball

soccer boots

golf tee

whistle

golf ball

Golf

caddie

golf hole

leisure shoes

Basketball

hoop

sweat suit top

basketball net

sweat suit bottoms

sneakers

Activities

tennis racket

weight lifter

headband

weight

tennis skirt

tennis player

Gymnastics

feet

legs

leotard

handstand

wristband

mat

sneakers

basketball

golf club

jump rope

flag

91

Action

smiling

kissing

hugging

hopping

sitting

eating

crossing legs

floating

blowing

pulling

licking

sitting

92

dangling

giggling

clapping

kneeling

standing

sitting

laughing

splashing

bending

Try this!

Fun action game

Think of a fun action word. Tell your friend what it is. Now, ask them to act it out. Take it in turns to play. You could . . .

. . . wriggle like a snake.

. . . or hop like a frog.

Guessing game

Think of the word for one of the pictures on these pages. When you've thought of it, find the word and cover it with a button or marker. Look for another word. Continue until you've covered all the circles.

You will need 34 buttons or markers

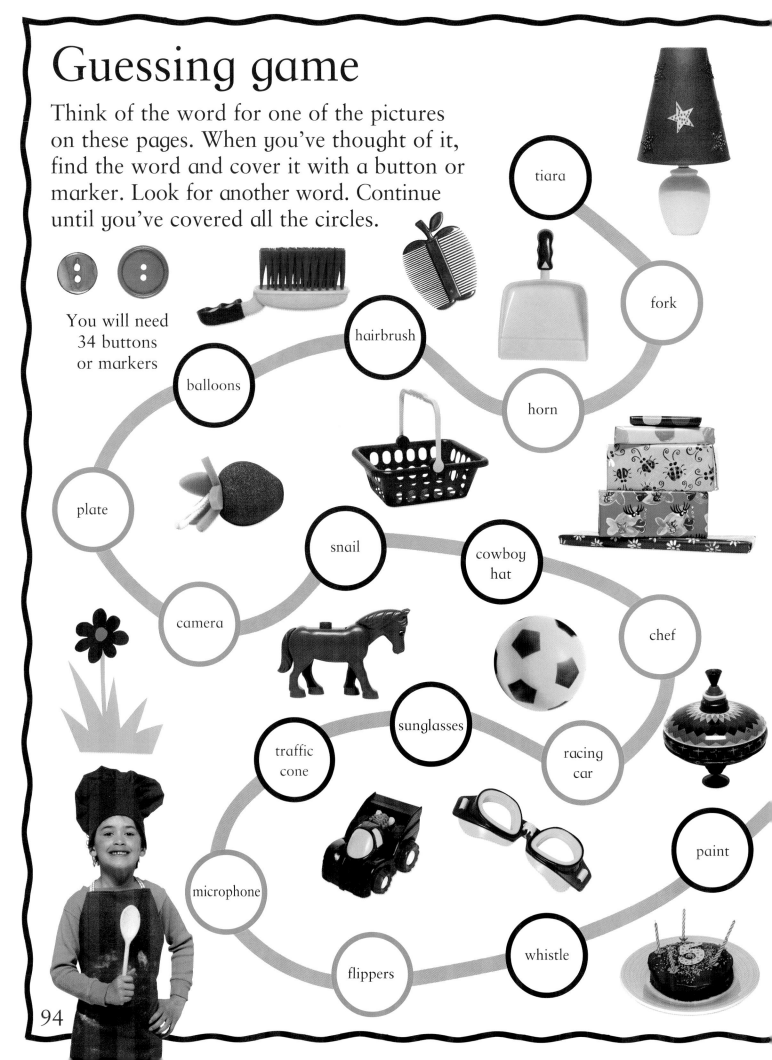

tiara

fork

hairbrush

balloons

horn

plate

snail

cowboy hat

chef

camera

sunglasses

racing car

traffic cone

paint

microphone

whistle

flippers

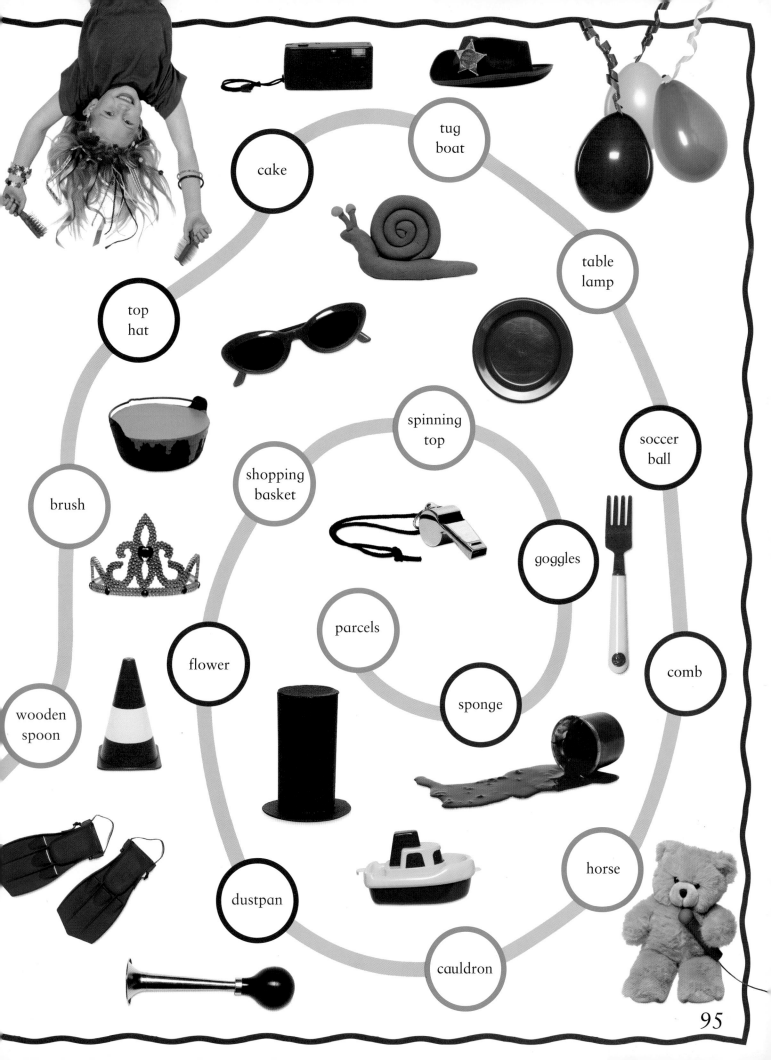

tug
boat

cake

table
lamp

top
hat

spinning
top

soccer
ball

shopping
basket

brush

goggles

parcels

flower

comb

wooden
spoon

sponge

horse

dustpan

cauldron

95

Try this!

Taste and tell game

1. Put some of these foods on a plate. Your friend must not see the food.

salty cracker

sweet, juicy apple

crisp lettuce

tasty cheese

spicy sausage

creamy yogurt

2. Blindfold your friend. Feed them each different food.

3. Can they name each food?

ANIMALS

Furry friends

Some animals have thick, soft fur to keep them warm. Others have hair or feathers that look like fur.

Hold on tight!

Long, skinny fingers help this raccoon to keep a tight grip.

Watch orang-utans swing through the trees – they do it with such ease!

These furry caterpillars will turn into moths.

Wolves howl loudly to one another to stay in touch.

Aroooo!

The tiny feathers on an ostrich's head look like fur!

It's easy for a squirrel to leap from tree to tree – its long, bushy tail keeps it balanced.

Try this!

Play the memory game

1. Think of all the furry animals you've seen at the zoo.
2. Start the game by saying, "I went to the zoo and I saw a polar bear."
3. The next person repeats this and adds another furry animal.
4. Take it in turns to repeat the sentence, adding another furry animal at each turn.

Thick, white fur coats keep these polar bears warm...

...as they snuggle up on the icy Arctic floor.

Tree kangaroos aren't like other kangaroos. They live up in the trees.

A red panda curls up for a snooze in the afternoon sun.

Fabulous feathers

Only one group of animals in the world has feathers. What is it? Yes, you've guessed it – birds!

Bzzz *Bzzz*

A pigeon takes off with a ... flap, flap, flap.

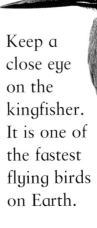

Here comes a bee! Where? Which way? Two hungry bee-eaters wait for lunch.

Bbbrrrrrr!
Bbbrrrrrr!

Did you know?

There are over 25,000 feathers on a single swan!

Emperor penguins live in freezing, frosty Antarctica. Layers of thick feathers protect them against biting cold winds.

Keep a close eye on the kingfisher. It is one of the fastest flying birds on Earth.

The puffin uses its bright beak to attract a mate in the summer.

Feathers keep the jay warm and also help it to fly.

A male bird of paradise shows off its long, beautiful feathers to impress its mate.

The brown pelican can hold masses of fish in its big, baggy bill.

The bald eagle isn't really bald. The feathers on its head are as white as snow!

Try this!

Make a bird t-shirt

1. Take a plain t-shirt. Draw a bird on it, with fabric paints.

2. Paint on bright feathers.

101

Wrinkly wonders

Thick, wrinkly skin may not look very pretty, but it is incredibly tough.

Ark! Ark!

A wrinkly rhinoceros sees off enemies with its sharp, curving horn.

Seals have a layer of fat underneath their skin to keep them extra warm.

Elephants are the largest land animals, and the only ones with trunks.

Huge hippos have little wrinkles.

Shar Pei dogs have very soft skin. It folds over and over, again and again.

Try this!

Make a wrinkly elephant

1. Draw a picture of an elephant and its tail. Cut them out.

2. Draw an eye. Glue on scrunched up pieces of tissue.

3. Attach the tail with a paper fastener, so that it swings.

The marabou stork does not have a voice box. It talks by making a hissing noise.

Hsss!
Hsss!

When the giant tortoise feels frightened, it hides its long flexible neck inside its solid shell.

The wildebeest keeps its head up and its beady eyes open, watching out for lions.

The Komodo dragon is the biggest lizard in the world.

The manatee pulls up plants from the river bed with its large, wrinkly snout.

Sssssssscaly

Scales give animals a tough top coat that protects them from wear and tear.

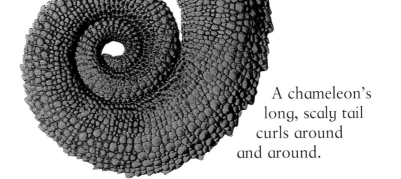

A chameleon's long, scaly tail curls around and around.

Try this!

Make a tropical fish

1. Draw the outline of an exotic fish on a piece of paper.

2. Cover it with bright scales made from shiny pieces of paper.

3. Give it an eye and draw on some waves and bubbles.

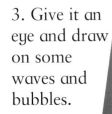

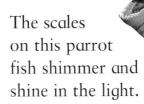

The scales on this parrot fish shimmer and shine in the light.

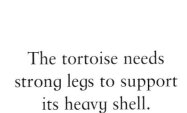

The tortoise needs strong legs to support its heavy shell.

Armadillos are covered in a strong, protective suit of scales.

Did you know?

Snakes shed their skin several times a year. Underneath is a new skin, in a larger size.

rattlesnake

A chameleon's sticky tongue can stretch twice as long as its body.

Watch out!

Sssslurp

Long, skinny toes...

...give lizards...

...a great grip.

A pangolin looks like a fir cone when it rolls into a ball. Its prickly scales keep it safe.

Snap! Snap!

Don't get too close! A baby crocodile has a big mouth and a painful bite.

Armadillos use their huge claws to dig deep down in the dirt for ants – their best snack!

Seeing spots

All sorts of animals are covered in spots. On some animals, the spots fade as the animal grows older.

A white-tailed deer fawn keeps its spots for two months. They help it to hide on the forest floor.

A snow leopard cub has a spotted coat, which hides it in the rocks and snow.

A ladybug's hard, shiny wing-cases have spots on them and protect its delicate wings.

These cheetah cubs will live with their mother until they are about a year and a half old. She teaches them how to stalk and catch their prey.

Try this!

Paint a butterfly picture

1. Paint half a butterfly on paper or card.

2. While the paint is wet, fold the paper, press hard and open it again. Do you have a perfect butterfly?

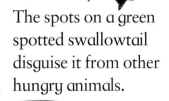

The spots on a green spotted swallowtail disguise it from other hungry animals.

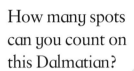

How many spots can you count on this Dalmatian?

These spotty, orange starfish are the size of dinner plates.

The rainbow boa glows a different shade with every little movement.

SSSSSSSS!

Geckos have no eyelids. They lick their eyes to keep them clean.

107

Simply stripy

Stripes stand out against this white page, but can be a clever disguise against trees, grass or leaves.

A Siberian tiger's stripes help it to hide as it silently stalks through the long grass.

Water dragons shed their skin, but they never lose their stripes!

A snail's shell is its mobile home. It goes wherever the snail goes.

The bright stripes on these caterpillars warn birds that they are not a tasty meal.

There is safety in numbers! Zebras travel in large herds for protection.

Over here!

One...

two...

...three African striped mice.

Ring-tailed lemurs signal to each other with their tails.

What is one way to tell that the copperhead is a poisonous snake?

Its bright red and orange stripes are a warning sign.

The okapi is a shy animal that does not like to be noticed. Its stripes help it to hide in the forest.

The zebra butterfly is named after another stripy animal – can you find it on this page?

When attacked, zebras run in different directions to confuse their attacker.

Daringly dazzling

Stunning brightness and interesting patterns make these animals the stars of the natural world.

Aren't I gorgeous?

Sssurprise!

The king bird of paradise sits on its throne, hoping to impress an admirer.

The green tree boa hides high in the trees. It drops on animals that pass below.

Bright yellow crab spiders hide on vivid yellow flowers.

Blue and yellow macaws stand out brightly in the dark rainforest.

Stay away!

This arrow poison frog's startling blue skin is a warning to hungry animals.

The blue morpho butterfly flutters from flower to flower, drinking sweet nectar.

The golden lion tamarin got its name because of its beautiful golden mane.

How does a tree frog balance on a stem? It has sticky suckers on its toes.

Golden beetles shine brightly in the sun, dazzling their enemies away.

The toucan's long, pointy bill is not as heavy as it looks. It is perfect for...

...picking fruit from branches.

Creepy-crawlies

Bugs live all around us. Some of them are living in your home or garden. Look for them under pots, stones or leaves.

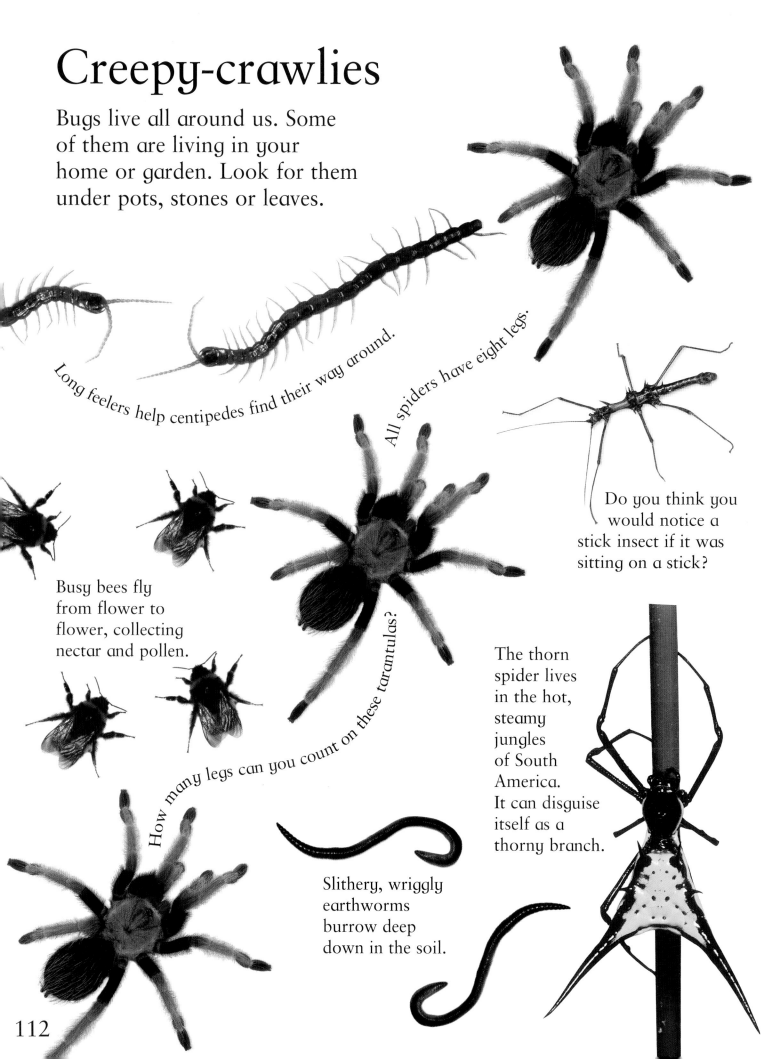

Long feelers help centipedes find their way around.

All spiders have eight legs.

Do you think you would notice a stick insect if it was sitting on a stick?

Busy bees fly from flower to flower, collecting nectar and pollen.

How many legs can you count on these tarantulas?

The thorn spider lives in the hot, steamy jungles of South America. It can disguise itself as a thorny branch.

Slithery, wriggly earthworms burrow deep down in the soil.

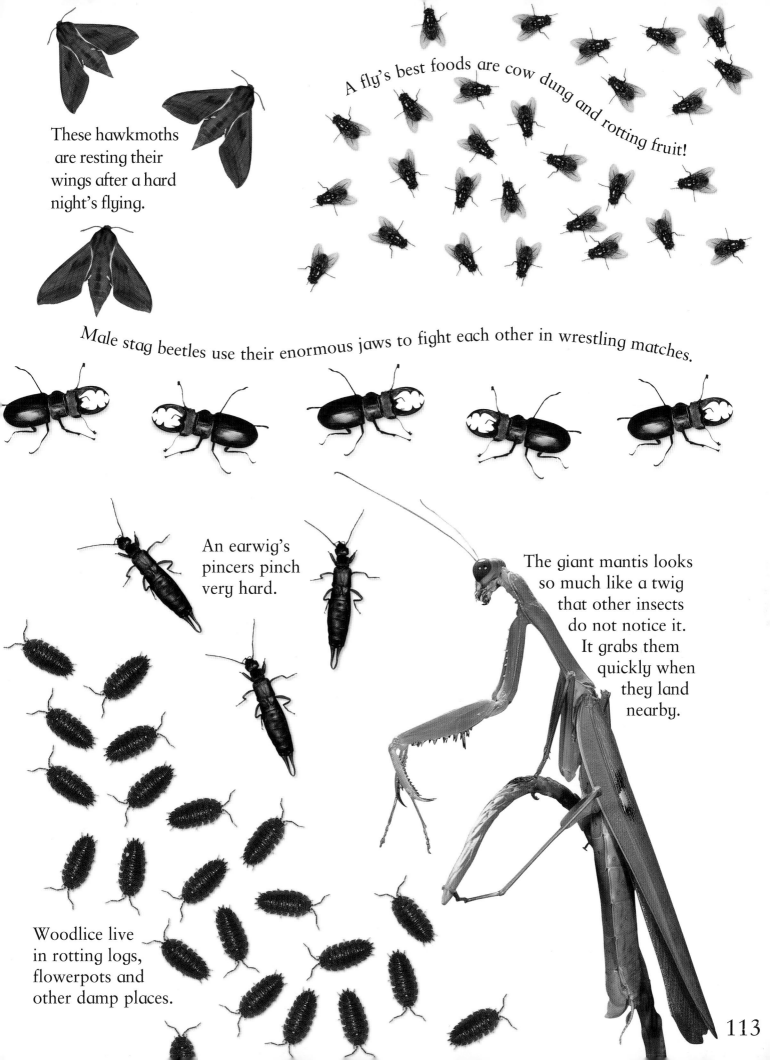

These hawkmoths are resting their wings after a hard night's flying.

A fly's best foods are cow dung and rotting fruit!

Male stag beetles use their enormous jaws to fight each other in wrestling matches.

An earwig's pincers pinch very hard.

The giant mantis looks so much like a twig that other insects do not notice it. It grabs them quickly when they land nearby.

Woodlice live in rotting logs, flowerpots and other damp places.

In the dark

Imagine you are out in the dark night. Which animals can you hear? Whose eyes are shining in the dark?

The loris has eyes like saucers.

They help it to see in the dark.

Sniff!

Prickly hedgehogs are shy animals. They come out at night for breakfast!

Sniff!

Try this!

Make a night scene

1. Cut out some bushes and trees. Stick them on a piece of black paper.

2. Add a silver Moon and a few twinkling stars.

3. Now add some eyes to shine in the dark. Which animal is hiding there?

Insects and worms are the kiwi's food of choice. It sticks its beak into the soil to sniff and smell them out.

114

Whooo!

Whooo!

Two barn owls take off for a night's hunting.

The flying fox is a bat that feeds on forest fruit at night. It sleeps upside down during the day.

Looking for a tasty dinner? Foxes visit parks and gardens, searching in garbage cans for food.

Badgers live in burrows underground. They come out at night to eat.

The mole lives in dark tunnels underground. It rarely sees the light of day.

The kakapo is a parrot that cannot fly. It crawls around at night.

Underwater

The ocean is home to many wonderful creatures that we rarely have a chance to see.

This beluga whale is curious about life above the sea.

Try this!

Underwater scene

1. To make some waves, cut two strips from tissue paper. Glue them at the top of a piece of blue paper.

2. Draw plants and rocks on the bottom of the paper. Glue on some shells. This is the seabed.

3. Draw in the creatures that live in your undersea kingdom.

The green sea turtle uses its paddles to push itself through the water.

The dainty European seahorse is actually no bigger than your hand!

Count the arms on these starfish. How many do they have?

116

Dolphins are playful animals that love to leap.

Splash!

Splish!

Beware!

When puffer fish feel threatened, they blow up into spiky balls.

Don't touch!

How many tentacles does an octopus have?

Crabs don't walk forwards; they scuttle sideways instead.

Grouper fish are covered with spots so that they blend into the coral reef.

117

Beautiful babies

Baby animals grow up quickly. They learn to copy what their parents do.

Baby bats are usually carried on their mother's tummy.

These bear cubs are looking for their mum. She's always somewhere close by.

Woof!

Woof!

This perky puppy wants to play.

Cheep!

Cheep!

Young chicks make a lot of noise! It helps their mothers find them.

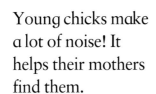

A seal pup is born on the ice. Its white furry coat keeps it warm and hides it against the snow.

Try this!

Can you find this koala's baby on the next page? Look through this section of the book and try to find parents for some of the other babies, too.

This baby lynx is learning to walk along a branch. It is holding on tightly with its claws.

Baby gorillas are curious creatures.

An albatross chick is an only child.

One day these ostrich chicks will grow into the biggest birds in the world.

Lion cubs are born with spotty coats which hide them in fields of long, dry grass.

A baby koala clings to its mother's back as she climbs through the trees.

Perfect pets

Many people's pets are their best friends. Do you have a pet at home? Can you find it on this page?

Mice have long, sensitive whiskers to help them feel things.

Squeak!

Squeak!

Budgies use their beaks to clean their feathers.

This long-eared rabbit is washing its face with its paws.

Hamsters nibble nuts and seeds. They gnaw at their cages, too!

Cats like to groom themselves after a meal.

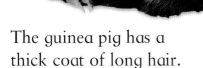

The guinea pig has a thick coat of long hair.

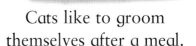

Gerbils are busy little animals. They hide in tubes, play on wheels and build themselves nests.

Try this!

Make a finger puppet mouse

1. Find or make a cardboard tube that fits on your finger. Then cut out a head, some ears, whiskers and a tail.

2. Fold the head and glue it to the end of the tube. Add the ears, whiskers and curly tail.

3. Add some eyes and give your mouse a name.

Goldfish flash and gleam as they dart around the tank.

Woof!
Woof!

A basset hound's best-loved time is walking time!

Do you have a field to spare?

A Shetland pony is a very small horse, but a very big pet.

Safari adventure game

Help Lucy the lion cub to find her mother. The winner is the first person to reach her. Take it in turns to roll a die and move your buttons or markers around the board. You will need:

buttons or markers

die

START

1

2

3

4 Crocodile won't let you pass. Go back to start.

5

6

7

8 Wait for panda to wake up and help you. Miss a go.

9

Sssssss!

10

Aroooo!

11 Wolf tells you about a short cut. Roll again.

12

13

14 Rainbow boa scares you. Go back five places.

Hold on tight!

18 Orang-utan gives you a lift. Move up two spaces.

19

20

21

22 Water dragon stops to talk to you. Miss a go.

17

Tsst! Tsst!

23

16

24

25

15

FINISH

26 Tortoise gives you a lift – the wrong way! Go back two spaces.

32

31

27

28

29

30 You chase two butterflies and get lost. Go back one space.

Try this!

Put the tail on the puppy

1. Paint a puppy and a tail on card or paper. Cut out the tail.

2. Press sticky tape on to the back of the tail. Fix the puppy to a wall.

3. Blindfold a friend. Spin them three times. Ask them to put the tail on the puppy.

SIZES

What size are you?

Tall, short, little, big – all of us have the same sort of shape, but we come in many different sizes.

I can *stretch myself out* wide.

I can hold myself in until I'm as thin as a pin.

Who is taller? You, or your friend? Take off your shoes, stand back-to-back, and see who is taller.

Massive Ted is much bigger than me.

Little Ted is smaller than me.

My legs don't stretch very far yet.

My legs are longer.

I have the longest legs of all three.

When you do a forward roll . . .

you go from tall . . .

to a small, tight ball.

Stretch up tall . . .   bend your knees . . .   crouch right down . . .   and tuck in your head.

Is your hair . . .

. . . short, . . .

. . . long, . . .

. . . or in-between?

Bigger and smaller than

Look around you each day to spot people, places and things that are bigger or smaller than each other.

An Afghan hound is much bigger than . . .

a Yorkshire terrier.

enormous present

smaller present

big rabbit ears

smaller cat's ears

My small lollipop will soon be gone.

My bigger lollipop will last all day long.

The small fish is after the big shark's tail. Uh-oh!

My big shopping bag is too heavy to lift.

My small handbag is light to carry.

Would you prefer a big bunch of flowers . . .

or a pretty little posy?

RUN!

You are much smaller than the dragon and his great big flames of fire.

These beads are small. I can hold dozens of them in my hands.

These beads are smaller. I can hold hundreds of them in my hands.

Have you heard the story of Pinocchio?

His nose grew bigger . . .

and bigger . . .

every time he told a lie.

Small, smaller, smallest

We sort small things in order of size: small, smaller and the smallest of them all.

small
ladybug

smaller
ladybug

smallest
ladybug

Small peas always seem to taste the sweetest.

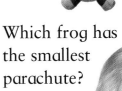

Which frog has the smallest parachute?

Three mice sailing across the salty sea.

Spotted fish swimming, one, two, three.

Try this!

Make three-size cookies

1. Buy some ready-made cookie dough. Find three cutters of different sizes.

2. Roll the dough flat with a rolling pin.

3. Cut out the cookies with the three cutters.

4. Bake in the oven until they are lovely and golden brown.

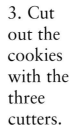

Can you sort these hats in order of size?

Big, bigger, biggest

Spot the **biggest** ballerina . . .

Long and short

Can you sort long things from short things?
Look at the objects on this page, then try
to find others at home.

short-tailed lizard

long-tailed lizard

Here is a short line of elephants waiting for a bus.

A super heroine
can fly off quickly
in a short cape.

A king walks
slowly in a
long cloak.

The bus has not arrived yet and the short line has become a long one.

Short socks cover
my ankles.

Long socks almost
reach my knees.

If you had a choice of long, slurpy
spaghetti strands or short pasta bows,
which would you want to eat?

Yum!
Yum!

Try this!

Make a slinky snake

1. Get nine paper cups and paint them.

 2. Take a cup for the head. Stick an eye on it.

3. Using a pencil, carefully make a hole in the bottom of the cup.

 4. Thread string through the hole and tie a knot.

 5. Join the cups together with paper fasteners.

 Pull your slinky snake along.

 Most cats have long tails, but the Manx cat has a short, stubby one.

long neck

If my neck was as long as a giraffe's, I could see high above the trees.

short neck

Did you know?

The giraffe's neck is longer than any other animal's.

Will you grow a moustache when you are older?

Will your hair be long or short?

133

Thick and thin

Would you choose the thick or thin things on this page? Is one better than the other?

Two monkeys are swinging on ropes.

Hey!

Which rope do you think will break?

Look at me!

Help yourself to a piece of cake. Which slice would you like?

The wizard's thick book of magic is full of weird and wonderful spells!

The teddy bears' book is thinner. A quick read!

Did you know?

Polar bears have thick fur coats to keep them warm in the cold.

How shall I wear my hair . . .

in two thick plaits . . .

or in lots of thin plaits?

Which spiders have the thickest legs?

A thick sweater warms you up on cold days.

A thin T-shirt keeps you cool on hot days.

This frog and squirrel are painting.

Are their paintings the same?

A thick rubber ring will help you to float in water.

Can you spin a hula-hoop around your waist?

Try this!

Thick and thin sandwiches

1. Ask an adult to cut four slices of bread – two thick and two thin. Butter them.

2. Ask for two slices of cheese – one thick and one thin.

3. Now ask for four slices of cucumber – two thick and two thin.

4. Make one very thick and one very thin sandwich.

Would you rather munch on a very thick sandwich or a very thin one?

thick sandwich   thin sandwich

Tall and short

There are tall and short things all around us.
Which ones are taller or shorter than you?

Are you taller than
your teddy bear?

Which of these
towers has
more beakers?

We need
a taller
ladder
to rescue
Chicken
from the
tower.
This short
ladder
will not
reach to
the top.

A dessert is a delicious
treat. Which one would
you choose
to eat?

Try this!

Who wears a hat?

1. Think of two people who wear hats. Draw them on a piece of paper.

2. Now think about their hats. Are they tall or short? Draw them on the picture.

3. Finish your picture with felt-tipped pens or crayons.

Pull out the sides of a bendy mirror and it will make you look short. Push in on the sides and you will look taller.

Look at these two teddy bear towers. Which one is taller?

Can you spot any differences between these two hats?

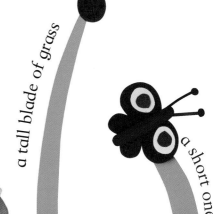

a tall blade of grass

a short one

137

Wide and narrow

Spotting whether things are wide or narrow is a way of seeing how much space they take up.

wide sunglasses   narrow sunglasses

wide tie   narrow tie

Stretching out to walk through a wide gap.

Squeezing through a narrow gap.

A mouse hole is wide enough for a tiny mouse but too narrow for a fat cat!

Which is the wide boat and which is the narrower boat?

wide blue sea

A big car needs four wide tyres.

A skinny bike only needs two narrow ones.

Lots of narrow bangles will easily fit on your arm.

How many wide bangles will fit on your arm?

Two elephants wobble along a narrow tightrope. Are they going to make it safely across?

Spiders scuttle along a wide plank.

Some ribbons are wide and silky. Others are narrow and fine.

Would you choose to wear . . .

narrow, clingy leggings . . .

or wide, baggy trousers (pants)?

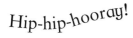

Hip-hip-hooray!

For an eye-popping finale . . .

stretch your arms out as wide as you can.

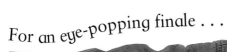

The same size

Two socks, two shoes, two gloves – when two things are the same size, we say that they make a pair.

A clown's shoes

Two shoes in the same size make a pair.

Ted is balancing on a pair of skis.

A scooter has two wheels that are just the same size.

Now he can slide down the snowy mountain slope.

Make sure that your roller skates are the same size!

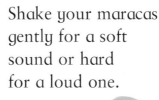

Some musical instruments come in pairs.

Crassh!

Crassh!

You need two cymbals to make a loud noise.

Shake your maracas gently for a soft sound or hard for a loud one.

Tsshh

Tsshh

140

Whose shoes?

A pair of shoes that tinkle and curl.
Who can they belong to?

Glittery party shoes

A perfect fit! The prince has finally found his princess.

Two cold hands need two woolly gloves.

Do you think these gloves will fit?

Look at yourself closely in the mirror.

You have two eyes and two ears just the same size.

What other parts of your body are the same size?

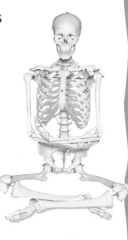
Did you know?

Your back relaxes and stretches out while you are sleeping at night. So, when you wake up you are a little bit taller than you were the day before.

141

Right size, wrong size

Are these children wearing the right-sized clothes?

It's important to have some things just the right size. You cannot ride a bike that is much too big, or wear shoes that are too small.

This chair is the right size.

Oops! This one isn't.

Try this!

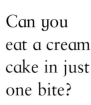

Make a paper doll

1. Draw a paper doll. It can be anything you want – an animal or a girl or a boy.

2. Lay see-through paper over the drawing. Draw some clothes for the doll.

3. Cut out the clothes and stick them on the doll. Do they fit?

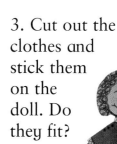

Can you eat a cream cake in just one bite?

A small mouthful of cheese is almost right.

A piece of popcorn is just the right size.

142

These shoes are the wrong size for me . . .

. . . but these shoes fit perfectly.

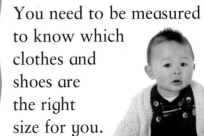
Two teddy bears are going for a ride.

Who has the right-sized bike?

Are these suitcases the right size?

too big

too small

The wrong-sized toothbrush.

Who is wearing the wrong-sized glasses?

The right-sized toothbrush.

143

growing UP

Our body changes as we get older. We grow taller and wider and we need bigger and bigger things.

A one-year-old baby can crawl.

A three-year-old toddler can walk and run.

An eight-year-old child can do things f-a-s-t!

Babies grow out of their clothes very quickly.

Toddlers learn how to dress themselves.

A bigger child needs bigger clothes.

A baby wears slippers to keep its feet warm.

A toddler's shoes slip on and off easily.

How old were you when you first tied your shoelaces?

Some babies are carried in safety chairs like this.

How old do you think the owner of this tricycle is?

Stabilizers will help you balance when you learn to ride a bike.

A 13-year-old teenager
is tall and strong.

At 25, you may have
stopped growing!

Try this!

See how you grow

1. Hang a big
piece of paper on
the wall. Stand in
front of it and ask
a friend to draw
around you.

2. When you
step away from
the paper, the
drawing will
show the shape
of your body.

3. Do the same
thing one month
later. Ask your
friend to draw
around you in
a different pen.

4. Take a ruler
and measure the
difference between
the two body
shapes. Have
you grown?

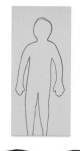

Whose shirt is this?

Do you like to wear
fashionable clothes?

Sneakers are easy and
comfortable to walk in.

High-heeled shoes are
harder to walk in.

When you are older,
you can ride on the road.

Only adults
are allowed
to ride a
motorbike.

145

Watch plants grOW...

Plants and animals are living things, too. Like people, they start life small but, as long as they have plenty of food, they soon begin to grow.

Small acorns grow on oak trees.

They fall to the ground in autumn (fall) and grow in the spring.

20 years later, the oak tree is as tall as a house, and still growing!

The young tree grows leaves in its first year.

Try this! Grow some sprouts

1. Soak some mung beans in water overnight. Drain them and leave in a covered jar.

2. After two days, the beans will start to sprout. Sprinkle them on top of a delicious salad.

Watch animals grow...

Baby animals grow more quickly than humans. In just a couple of months, they may be ten times bigger than when they were born.

When kittens are born, their mother licks them clean.

Even after one week a kitten's eyes are still tightly closed.

At three weeks, the kitten has started to move around. But it is still not very strong.

Nine weeks old, and the kitten is almost ready for its first trip outside.

This puppy is three days old. It only sleeps and eats.

Three weeks old, and the puppy is becoming more active.

At five weeks, puppies begin to be curious about the world around them.

After eight weeks the puppies are ready to go to a new home.

This baby owl is resting after hatching out of its shell.

A group of two-week-old owlets wait for a meal.

Four weeks old, and the owlets are moving around their nest.

After twelve weeks, an owlet loses its fluffy feathers and is growing fast.

147

Spot the size

Take it in turns to throw the die and move your button around the board. When you land on a square, look for the answers on the page. You have ten seconds to do this. If you can't, miss a turn. If you can, you have another go. The first one to finish is the winner.

You will need 2 buttons or markers, a timer and a die.

START

1 Find another ladybug of the same size.

2 Just how big can his nose grow? Find an even bigger one.
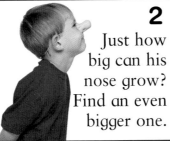

3 Find me with my blown-up balloon.

4 I've got thin legs. Find the spider with thicker legs.

10 Find someone with a short moustache.
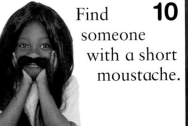

9 Find a wide bangle.

5 Find the smallest frog.

6 Find a lizard with a long tail.

7 Find a tall dessert.

8 Find a bigger ted.

13

Find a
shorter tower.

14

Find a longer
blade of grass.

15

I was
thinner
before I
ate that cheese. Where
is the thinner me?

16

Find a
narrower
boat.

11

Find a
thicker
sandwich.

12

Find the same
size boot.

17

Find an older
kitten.

FINISH

21

Find
someone
who is
stretching
out wide.

20

These shoes are too
big – find me a pair
that will fit properly.

19

Find the
wrong-sized
toothbrush.

18

Whoops! Elephant
has sat on the wrong
chair. Find the right-
sized chair for him.

149

Try this!

Make a picture puzzle

1. Draw a picture on a piece of thin card. Paint it brightly.

2. On the back, draw four or five wiggly lines across the card.

3. Cut the card into pieces along the lines.

4. Ask a friend to put the puzzle pieces back together again.

COUNTING

Pairs

A pair is two things that go together and look the same.

This is a pair of shoes.

Can you find all the pairs of things on this page?

How many pairs of shoes do you have?

Can you think of any other pairs?

How many pairs of socks would an elephant need?

Try this!

Sorting socks

1. Draw lots of socks.

2. Now cut them out.

3. Paint each pair with a different pattern. Hang them on a washing line.

152

Partners

Partners are two things that go
together, but do not look the same.

A bat and ball
are partners.

Can you find
all the partners
on this page?

What goes with
a scarf to keep
you warm?

What do you use
with a knife to
help you eat?

What do you
think the
puppy is
waiting for?

153

Colours

How many colours can you see?
Can you match the things that
are the same colour?

yellow

blue

red

cuddly
octopus

jumping
frog

toy boat

weird alien

creepy crab

floating bath ducks

wobbly
skittles

smiling girl

long, long gloves

Did you know?

The colours red, orange,
yellow, green, blue,
indigo and violet make
a rainbow!

154

Patterns

How many patterns can you see? Match the things that have the same pattern.

spotty

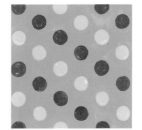

checked

stripy

snuggly tiger

beach bucket

balloons

great big ladybug

summer shorts

pretty spoon

woolly teddy bear

snazzy trousers (pants)

bright dice

Look at my face!

Can you paint different patterns?

big plate

155

Numbers are everywhere

There are numbers all around you.
Which numbers can you see?

39

toy cooker

How much do these
pears cost?

wristwatches

long
ruler

pocket
calculator

How many numbers can you see on a telephone?

clown clock

bright dartboard

shiny blue
telephone

sports
shirt

animal
dominoes

Number parade

Join the number parade! Can you count the funny faces?

0   no faces at all!

1  one stripy tiger

How many animals are at the farm? Can you count...

1 horse?   4 sheep?   5 goats?

2 cows?   3 pigs?

2  two glittery tiaras

Can you count the spots on the smilers' faces?

3  three spotty smilers

How many pirates can you see?

4  four silly moustaches

5  five jolly pirates

0 1 2 3 4 5

From six to ten

There are a lot more faces to see. This number parade goes up to ten!

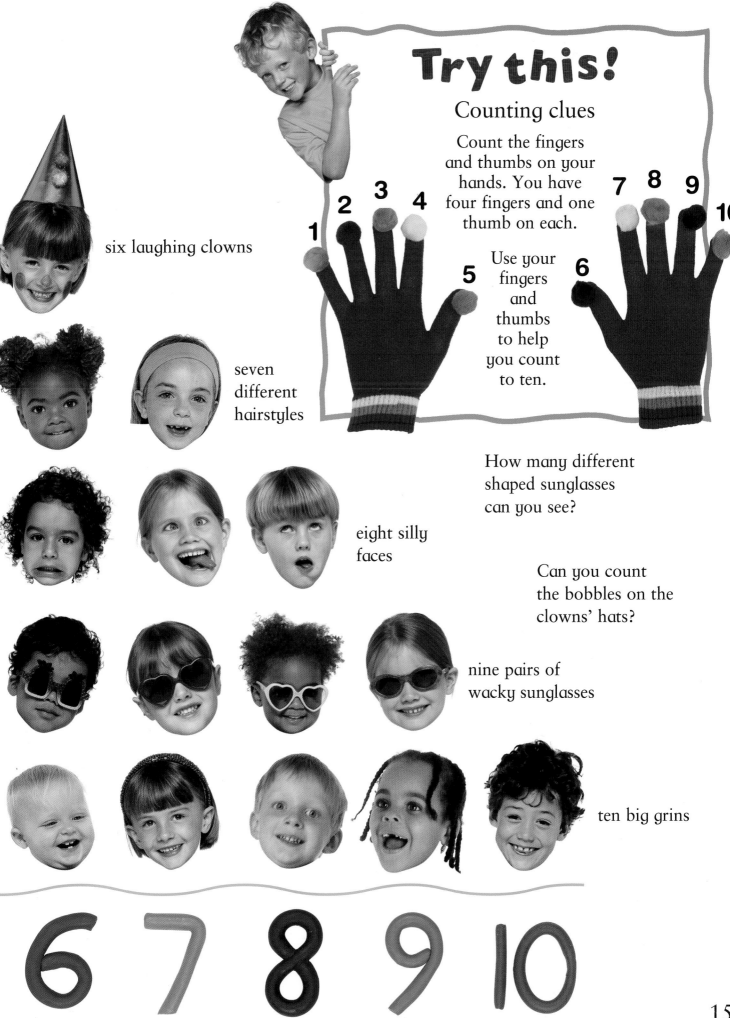

Try this!

Counting clues

Count the fingers and thumbs on your hands. You have four fingers and one thumb on each.

Use your fingers and thumbs to help you count to ten.

1 2 3 4 5 6 7 8 9 10

six laughing clowns

seven different hairstyles

eight silly faces

How many different shaped sunglasses can you see?

Can you count the bobbles on the clowns' hats?

nine pairs of wacky sunglasses

ten big grins

6 7 8 9 10

Countdown

Can you count back down to zero? Use your fingers and thumbs to help.

When rockets are launched into Space, a computer counts down to blast off.

Did you know?

The Moon is about 384,400km/ 238,855 miles away from the Earth, but you can still see it!

Goodbye Space Ted! Will you help me count down to zero?

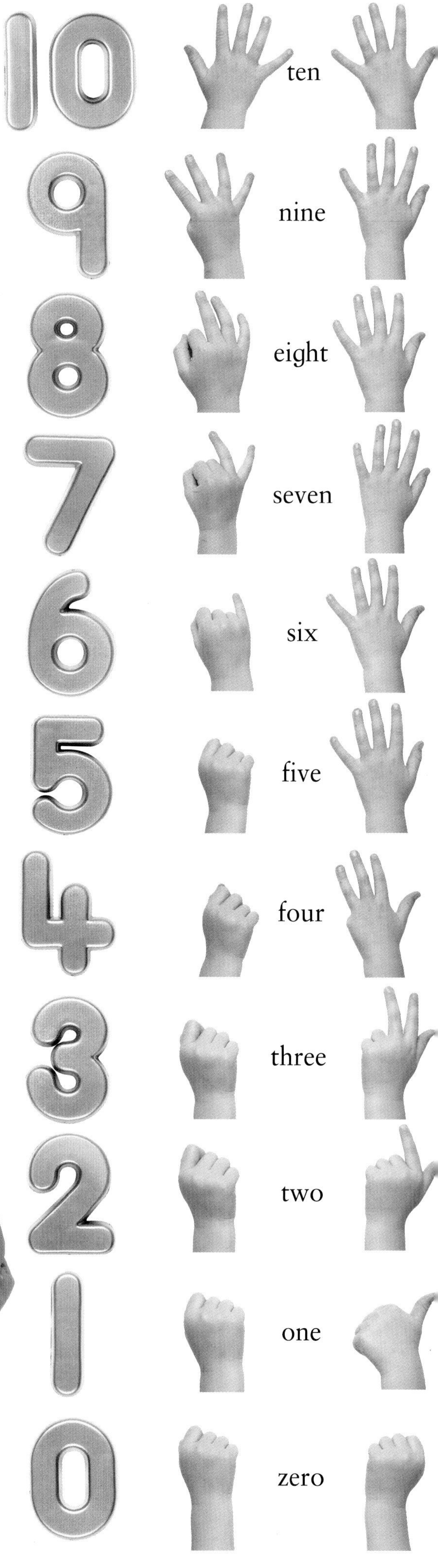

ten

nine

eight

seven

six

five

four

three

two

one

zero

How many?

You can count all sorts of things. How many…

…dancing pigtails?

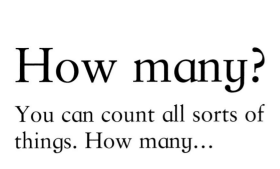

…eyes?

…ears?

…noses?

…mouths?

…legs on a bumble bee?

…stripes on the iguana's tail?

…crossed-over legs?

…goldfish in a bowl?

…fingers and thumbs?

…wiggly toes?

Try this!

Family numbers

Draw 2 eyes…   2 ears…

1 nose…   a pair of lips…

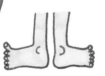

2 feet…   2 hands…

…for everyone in your family. Keep a notebook of your family numbers.

Party numbers

Tom is three today, and Jessica is five years old. Can you find all the numbers that match their ages?

How many chocolate drops are on this cookie?

1 •

2 ••

3 •••

4 ••••

5 •••••

Are these balloons for Jessica?

How many presents can you count?

Who would have these cherries?

Who will wear this birthday badge?

Is this birthday card for Tom?

Jessica is five years old.

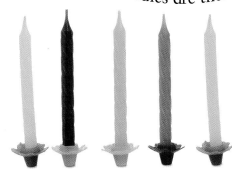

Whose birthday candles are these?

Try this!

Make birthday badges

1. Cut out small circles of card.

2. Decorate with a number.

3. Hang your badges on a ribbon or attach a safety pin at the back.

4. Make a badge for everyone in your family.

How many candles?

Who will wear this badge?

Can you count these presents?

How many balloons are here?

Are there five chocolate drops on this cookie?

Who is this birthday card for?

Tom is three years old.

6

7

8

9

10

Are they the same?

Can you tell if there are the same number of things? Count them and see.

Are there the same number of chocolate bars as ice creams?

Are there the right number of hats for all the children?

Try this!

Make a teddy bears' picnic

1. Find 3 bears or other toys.

2. Find 3 plates.

3. Find 3 cups.

4. Find 3 spoons.

5. Make play food.

6. Give each teddy the same amount of play food on a plate.

Are there enough plates of food for all the children?

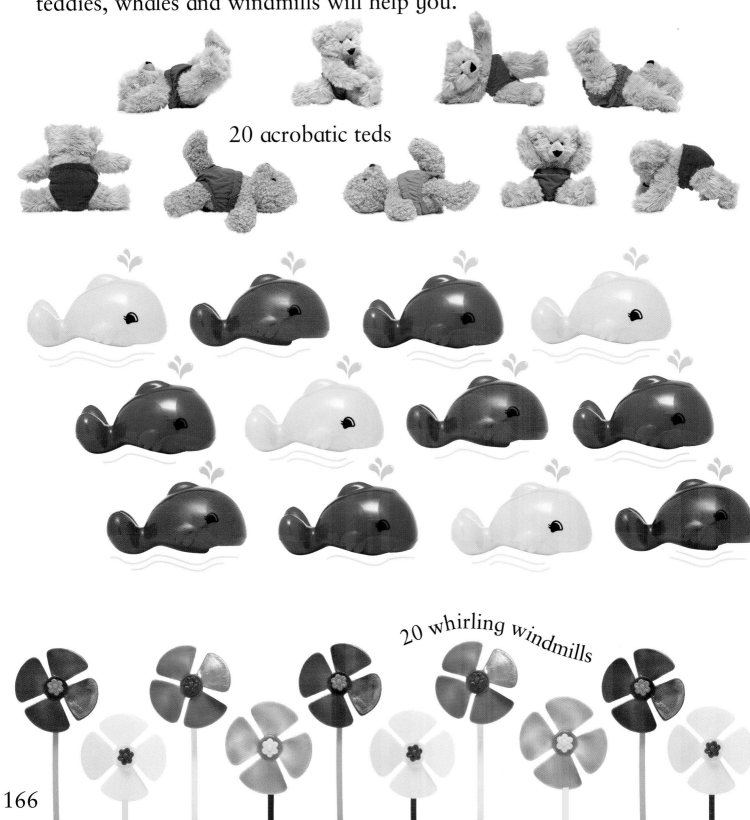

Up to twenty

Can you count all the way up to 20? These teddies, whales and windmills will help you.

20 acrobatic teds

20 whirling windmills

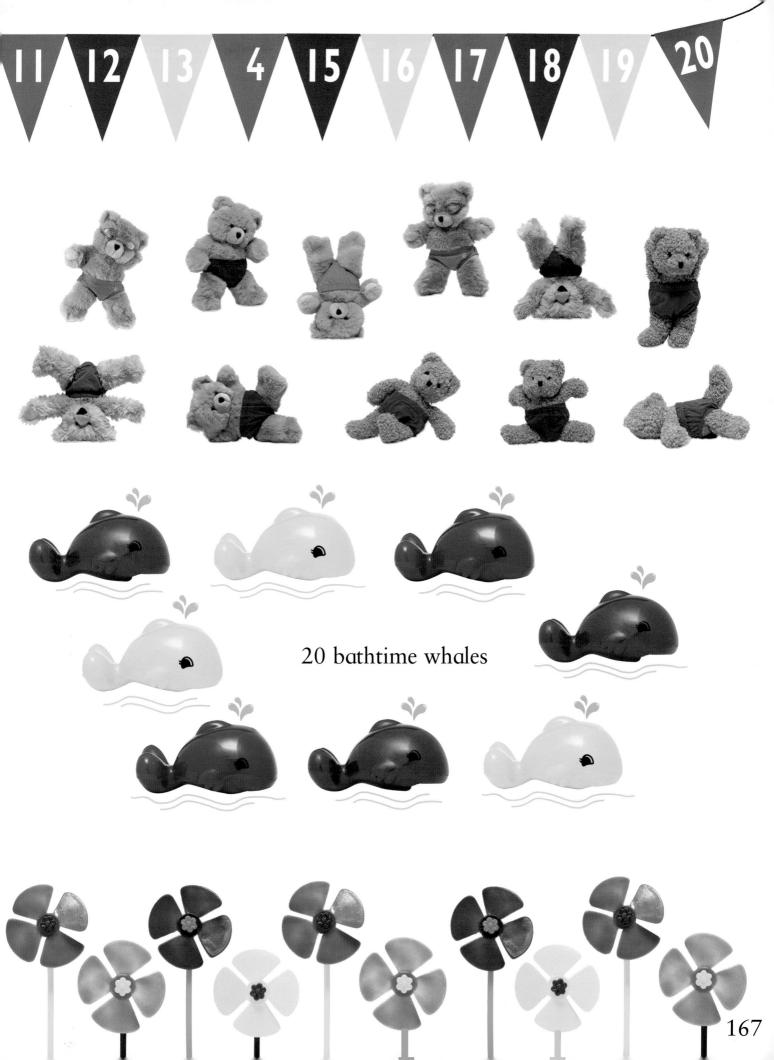

20 bathtime whales

167

10 Great big numbers

Numbers just keep getting bigger!
Can you count these great big numbers?

Can you count 10 shapes?

Can you count 20 circles?

20

Can you count 30 squares?

30

Can you count 50 sequins?

Can you count 60 bobbles?

40

Can you count 90 semi-circles?

Can you count 80 ovals?

50

Can you count 40 shapes?

Can you count 70 triangles?

Can you count 100 stars?

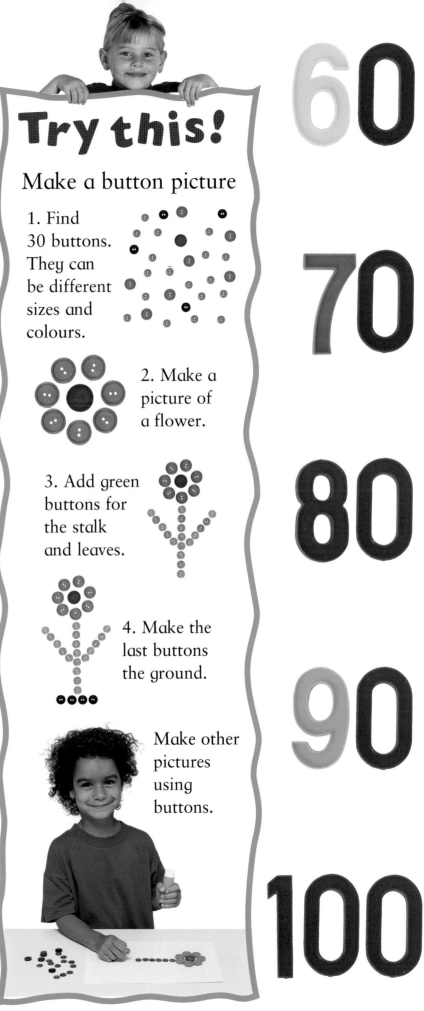

Try this!

Make a button picture

1. Find 30 buttons. They can be different sizes and colours.

2. Make a picture of a flower.

3. Add green buttons for the stalk and leaves.

4. Make the last buttons the ground.

Make other pictures using buttons.

60

70

80

90

100

169

Party game

Bill and Bob are going to Teddy's birthday party. Do you want to come too? You will need one die and a button or marker for each player.

markers or buttons

die

START

Bob

Bill

1

2

3

4

5
You fall in a puddle. Go back to START and have a wash.

6

7

8

9
You have forgotten the cake. Go back to START to make one.

10

11

12

13

14
You have found some flowers. Have an extra go.

15

16

17

18

24

25
You are very excited. Run forward 3 spaces.

26

23

27
Tie the bow on your present. Go back 4 spaces.

22

21
Stop for a snack. Miss a turn.

28

29

30

20

19

FINISH

Try this!

Make a height chart

Stand in front of a piece of paper sticky taped to a wall. Ask a friend to mark your height. Wait a month before your height is marked again. Have you grown?

MATHS

Are there enough?

Four toys are going to the seaside. They are taking all these different things. Do they have enough, too many or too few?

Are there enough sandwiches for all the toys?

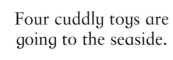

Does each toy have a bag?

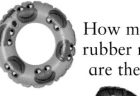

Do the toys all have surfboards to ride the waves?

Four cuddly toys are going to the seaside.

How many rubber rings are there?

Can you count the swimming goggles?

Count the towels. Are there enough?

Are there the same number of inflatable rafts as there are toys?

The toys like swimming. Do they have enough snorkels?

Is there a swimming cap for everyone?

174

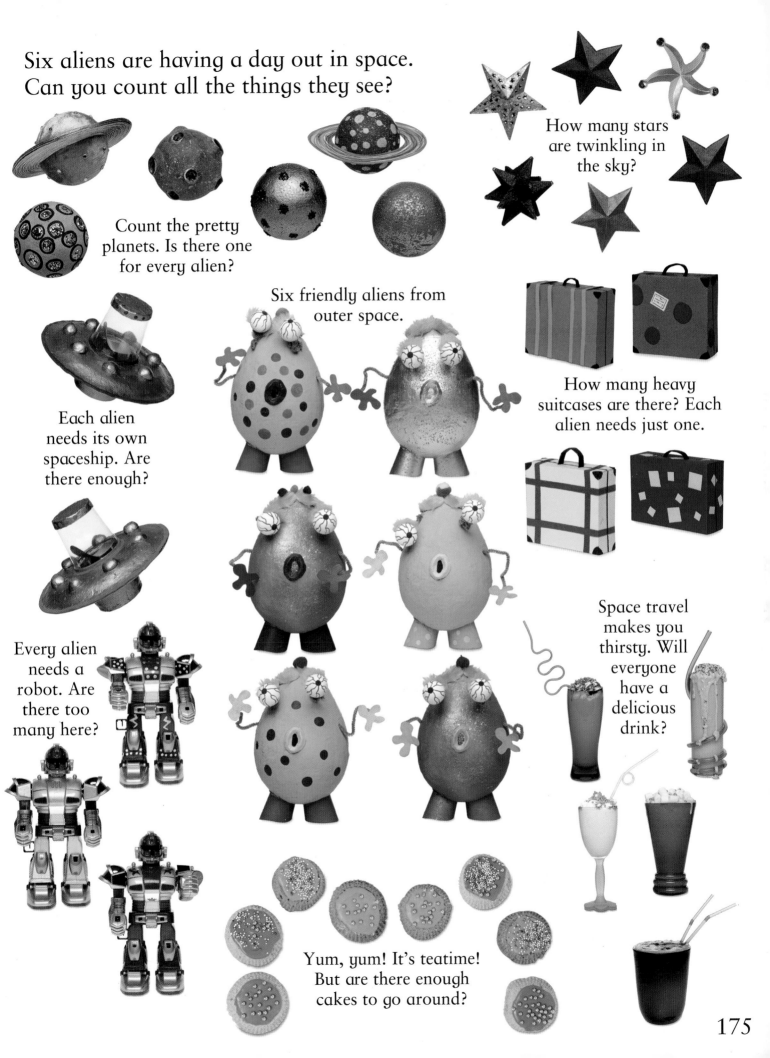

Six aliens are having a day out in space.
Can you count all the things they see?

How many stars
are twinkling in
the sky?

Count the pretty
planets. Is there one
for every alien?

Six friendly aliens from
outer space.

How many heavy
suitcases are there? Each
alien needs just one.

Each alien
needs its own
spaceship. Are
there enough?

Every alien
needs a
robot. Are
there too
many here?

Space travel
makes you
thirsty. Will
everyone
have a
delicious
drink?

Yum, yum! It's teatime!
But are there enough
cakes to go around?

How many altogether?

When you add two things together you can make a sum. In a sum, you use numbers and signs instead of words.

This sign means add together.

This sign means equals.

This is how you write the sum.

1+2=3

1 teddy acrobat

2 more teddy acrobats

3 teddy acrobats altogether

This is how you write the sum.

2+0=2

2 circus clowns

0 clowns

2 circus clowns altogether

This is how you write the sum.

4+1=5

4 teddies on a scooter

1 more teddy on a scooter

5 teddies altogether

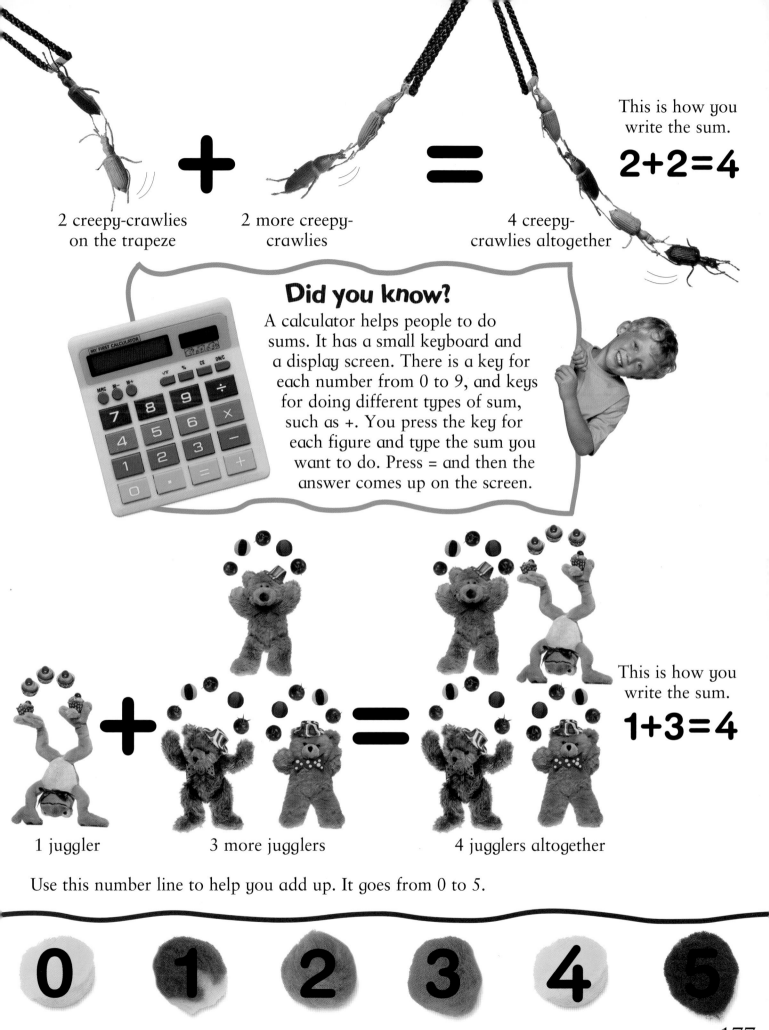

2 creepy-crawlies on the trapeze

2 more creepy-crawlies

4 creepy-crawlies altogether

This is how you write the sum.

2+2=4

Did you know?

A calculator helps people to do sums. It has a small keyboard and a display screen. There is a key for each number from 0 to 9, and keys for doing different types of sum, such as +. You press the key for each figure and type the sum you want to do. Press = and then the answer comes up on the screen.

1 juggler

3 more jugglers

4 jugglers altogether

This is how you write the sum.

1+3=4

Use this number line to help you add up. It goes from 0 to 5.

0   1   2   3   4   5

Adding up

This page is full of children and toys enjoying a party with their friends. Can you do all the adding up sums?

This sign means add together.

This sign means equals.

 **+**  **=**

This is how you write the sum.

5+2=7

5 presents

2 more presents

7 presents altogether

This is how you write the sum.

6+0=6

6 dancing toys

0 toys

6 dancing toys altogether

Try this!

Draw the sum shown below on a piece of paper. How many clowns and jugglers are there altogether?

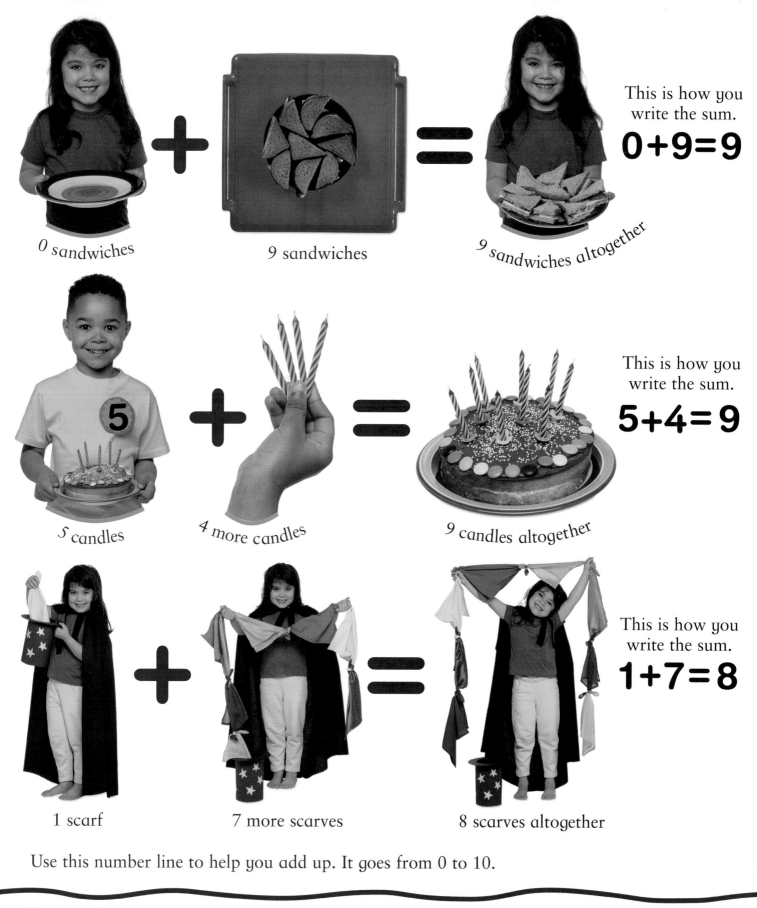

0 sandwiches + 9 sandwiches = 9 sandwiches altogether

This is how you write the sum.

0+9=9

5 candles + 4 more candles = 9 candles altogether

This is how you write the sum.

5+4=9

1 scarf + 7 more scarves = 8 scarves altogether

This is how you write the sum.

1+7=8

Use this number line to help you add up. It goes from 0 to 10.

0 1 2 3 4 5 6 7 8 9 10

Practise adding up

These creepy crawlies are busy working, eating, crawling and flying. How many are there in each sum?

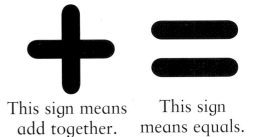

This sign means add together.

This sign means equals.

This is how you write the sum.

8+10=?

8 hungry flies

10 more flies

How many flies altogether?

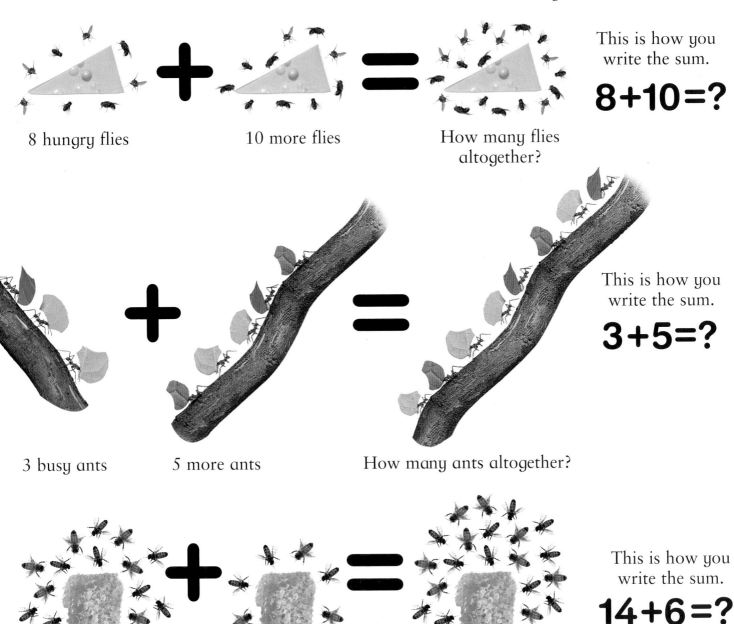

This is how you write the sum.

3+5=?

3 busy ants

5 more ants

How many ants altogether?

This is how you write the sum.

14+6=?

14 buzzy bees

6 more bees

How many bees altogether?

Use this number line to help you add up. It goes all the way from 0 to 20.

0 1 2 3 4 5 6 7 8 9 10

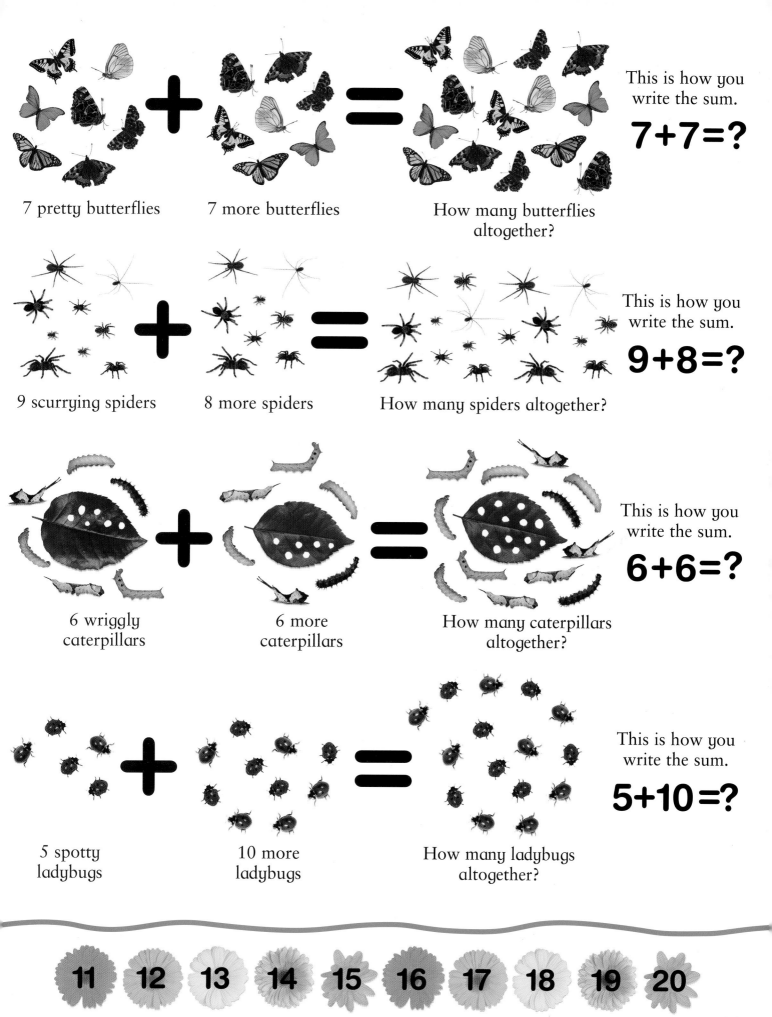

7 pretty butterflies

7 more butterflies

How many butterflies altogether?

This is how you write the sum.

7+7=?

9 scurrying spiders

8 more spiders

How many spiders altogether?

This is how you write the sum.

9+8=?

6 wriggly caterpillars

6 more caterpillars

How many caterpillars altogether?

This is how you write the sum.

6+6=?

5 spotty ladybugs

10 more ladybugs

How many ladybugs altogether?

This is how you write the sum.

5+10=?

11 12 13 14 15 16 17 18 19 20

How many are left?

To work out the difference between two sets of numbers, we take one away from the other. This is another sort of sum, it is called taking away.

 This sign means take away.

 This sign means equals.

This is how you write the sum.

5-2=3

5 ice creams   The teds take 2 away   3 ice creams are left

This is how you write the sum.

2-2=0

2 rubber rings   Swimmers take 2 away   0 rubber rings are left

  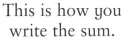 

This is how you write the sum.

5-1=4

5 books in a pile   The teds take 1 to read   4 books are left

This is how you write the sum.

3-2=1

3 teds on a scooter   2 teds fall off   1 ted is left

1 cookie on
a pillow

Ted eats 1

0 cookies are left

This is how you
write the sum.

1-1=0

Did you know?

An abacus was the first sort of
calculator. It is still
used in some countries
to work out sums.

3 toys are flying kites

1 toy floats off

2 toys are left

This is how you
write the sum.

3-1=2

4 farmers at work

2 farmers go home

2 farmers are left

This is how you
write the sum.

4-2=2

Use this number line to help you take away. It goes from 0 to 5.

0   1   2   3   4   5

Taking away

There are lots of hungry animals on this page. Work out how much food they have eaten and how much food is left.

This sign means take away.

This sign means equals.

This is how you write the sum.

8-1=7

8 bananas hanging on a tree

Monkey takes 1

7 bananas are left

This is how you write the sum.

10-5=5

10 sweet apples

Tortoise eats 5

5 apples are left

This is how you write the sum.

7-5=2

7 chunks of tasty cheese

Mouse eats 5

2 chunks are left

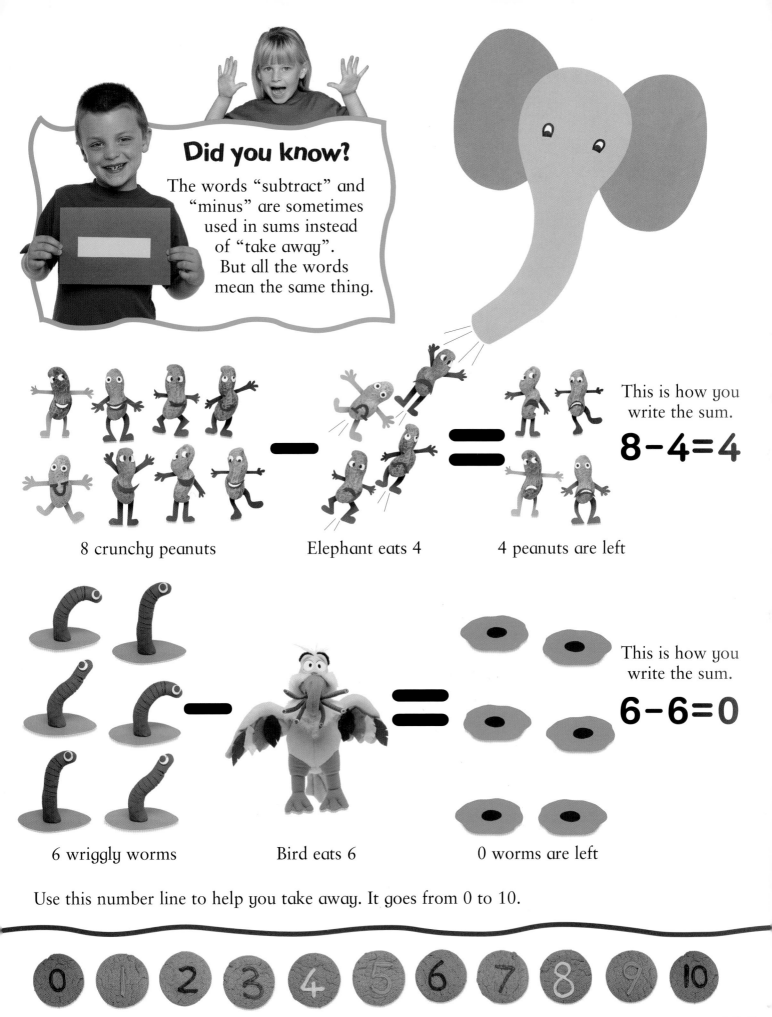

Did you know?

The words "subtract" and "minus" are sometimes used in sums instead of "take away". But all the words mean the same thing.

This is how you write the sum.

8-4=4

8 crunchy peanuts

Elephant eats 4

4 peanuts are left

This is how you write the sum.

6-6=0

6 wriggly worms

Bird eats 6

0 worms are left

Use this number line to help you take away. It goes from 0 to 10.

0 1 2 3 4 5 6 7 8 9 10

Practise taking away

Here is a chance for you to practise some more take away sums. Can you work out the answers to these?

This sign means take away.

This sign means equals.

This is how you write the sum.

9-9=?

9 cookies on a plate

A hungry girl takes 9

How many cookies are left?

This is how you write the sum.

6-1=?

6 musical instruments

A musician takes 1

How many instruments are left?

This is how you write the sum.

11-4=?

11 frogs balancing

4 frogs fall off

How many frogs are left?

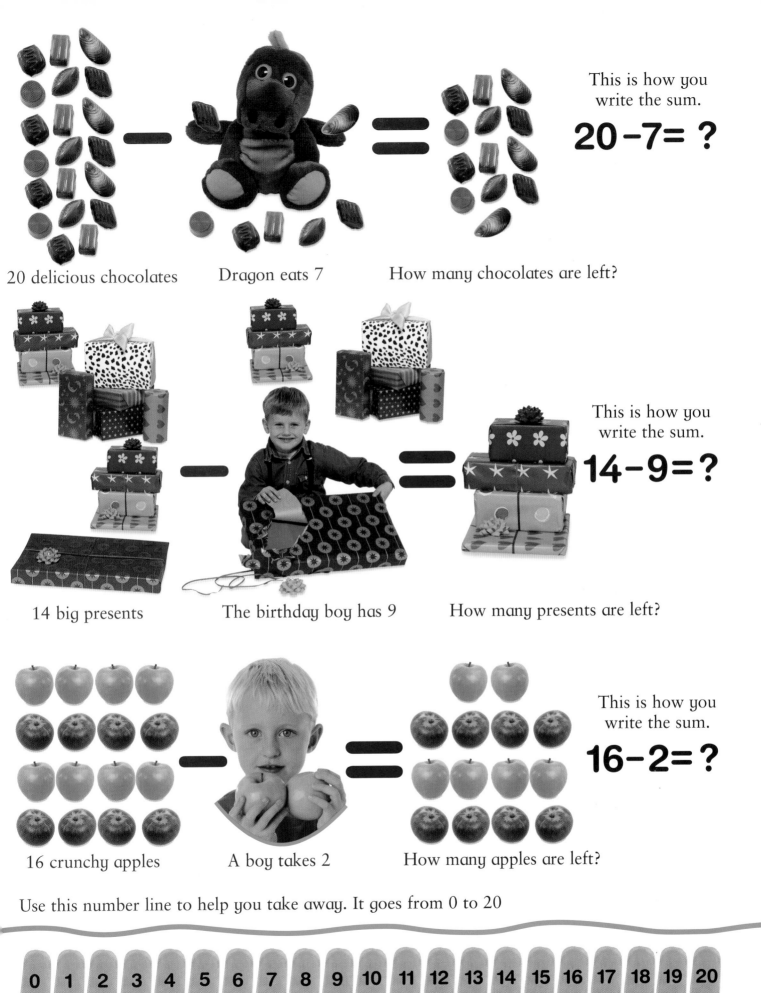

20 delicious chocolates Dragon eats 7 How many chocolates are left?

This is how you write the sum.

20 – 7 = ?

14 big presents The birthday boy has 9 How many presents are left?

This is how you write the sum.

14 – 9 = ?

16 crunchy apples A boy takes 2 How many apples are left?

This is how you write the sum.

16 – 2 = ?

Use this number line to help you take away. It goes from 0 to 20

0 1 2 3 4 5 6 7 8 9 10 11 12 13 14 15 16 17 18 19 20

How many times?

Sometimes you have to count groups of things.
Multiplying is quick way of counting them.
For this kind of sum we use the times sign.

This sign means times.   This sign means equals.

There are 2 children   Each child has 2 legs   There are 4 legs altogether

This is how you write the sum.

2×2=4

There are 3 children   Each child has 2 arms   There are 6 arms altogether

This is how you write the sum.

3×2=6

Each hat has 5 bobbles   There are 3 hats   There are 15 bobbles altogether

This is how you write the sum.

5×3=15

188

Try this!

Find a few pairs of gloves and socks, and lay them on the floor. How many gloves and socks are there altogether? Try making some more sums using the x sign.

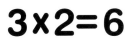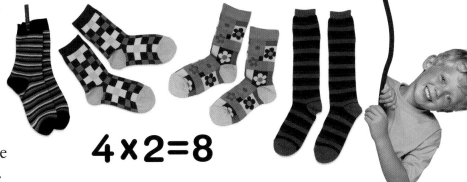

4 x 2 = 8

3 x 2 = 6

This is how you write the sum.

4 x 2 = 8

There are 4 pairs of socks   Each pair has 2 socks   There are 8 socks altogether

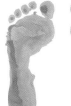

This is how you write the sum.

5 x 2 = 10

There are 5 pairs of feet   Each pair has 2 feet   There are 10 feet altogether

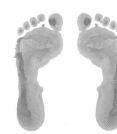

This is how you write the sum.

4 x 5 = 20

How many rings?   There are 4 hands   Each hand has 5 rings   There are 20 rings altogether

189

More times

All the things on this page are arranged in groups. Try doing the times sums to find out how many things there are altogether.

This sign means times. This sign means equals.

There are 2 lines of fish

There are 4 fish in each line

This is how you write the sum.

2×4=8

There are 3 groups of starfish

There are 10 starfish in each group

This is how you write the sum.

3×10=30

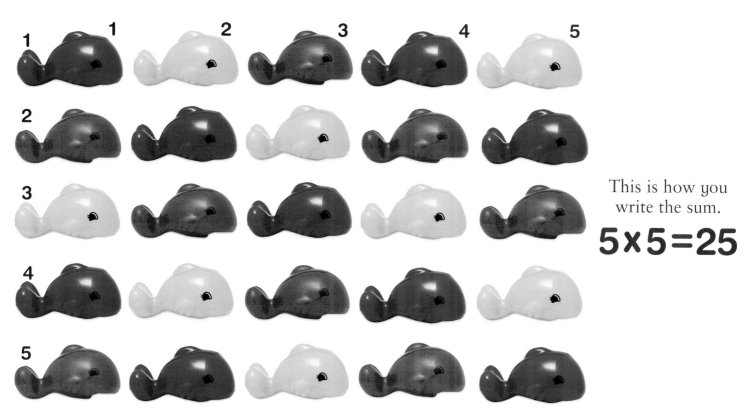

There are 5 rows of whales

There are 5 whales in each row

This is how you write the sum.

5×5=25

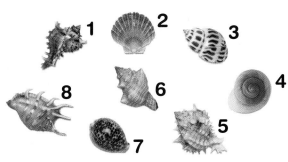 

This is how you write the sum.

2x8=16

There are 2 groups of shells   There are 8 shells in each group

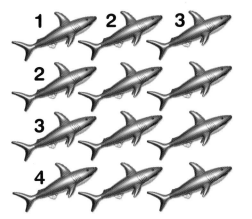 

This is how you write the sum.

5x6=30

There are 5 groups of lobsters   There are 6 lobsters in each group

This is how you write the sum.

2x12=24

There are 2 groups of sharks   There are 12 sharks in each group

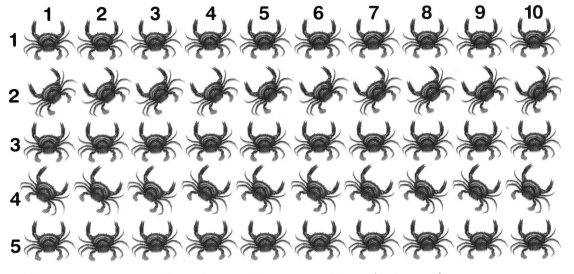

This is how you write the sum.

5x10=50

There are 5 rows of crabs   There are 10 crabs in each row

Times tables

You'll soon start to learn your times tables. Knowing them off by heart helps you to do sums *F-A-S-T*.

× This sign means times.

= This sign means equals.

1 x 1 = 1
2 x 1 = 2
3 x 1 = 3
4 x 1 = 4
5 x 1 = 5
6 x 1 = 6
7 x 1 = 7
8 x 1 = 8
9 x 1 = 9
10 x 1 = 10

4 x 1 = ?

1 x 2 = 2
2 x 2 = 4
3 x 2 = 6
4 x 2 = 8
5 x 2 = 10
6 x 2 = 12
7 x 2 = 14
8 x 2 = 16
9 x 2 = 18
10 x 2 = 20

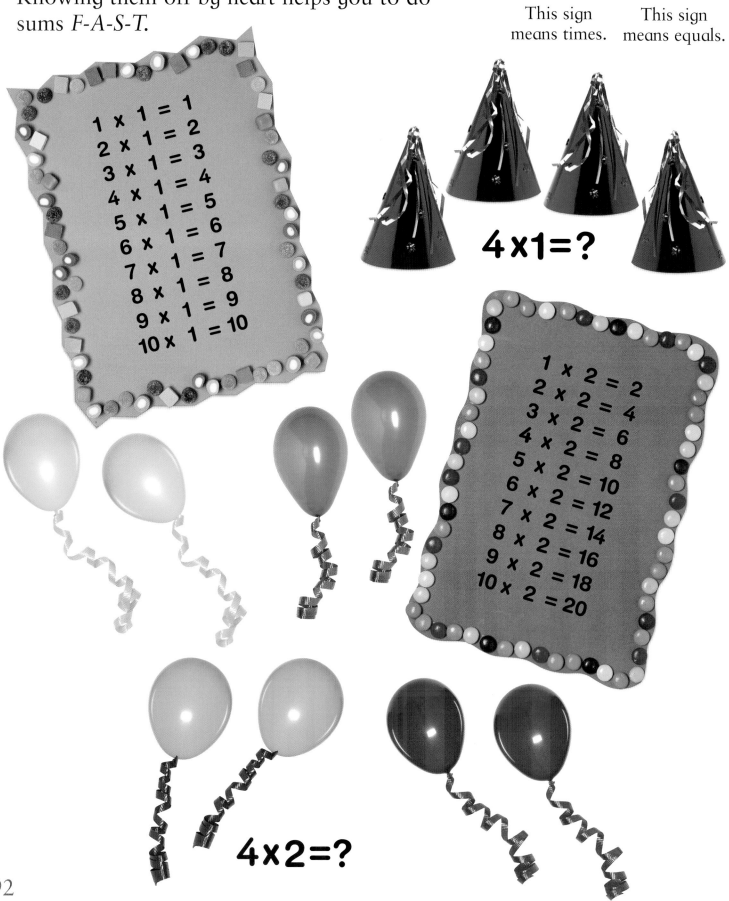

4 x 2 = ?

192

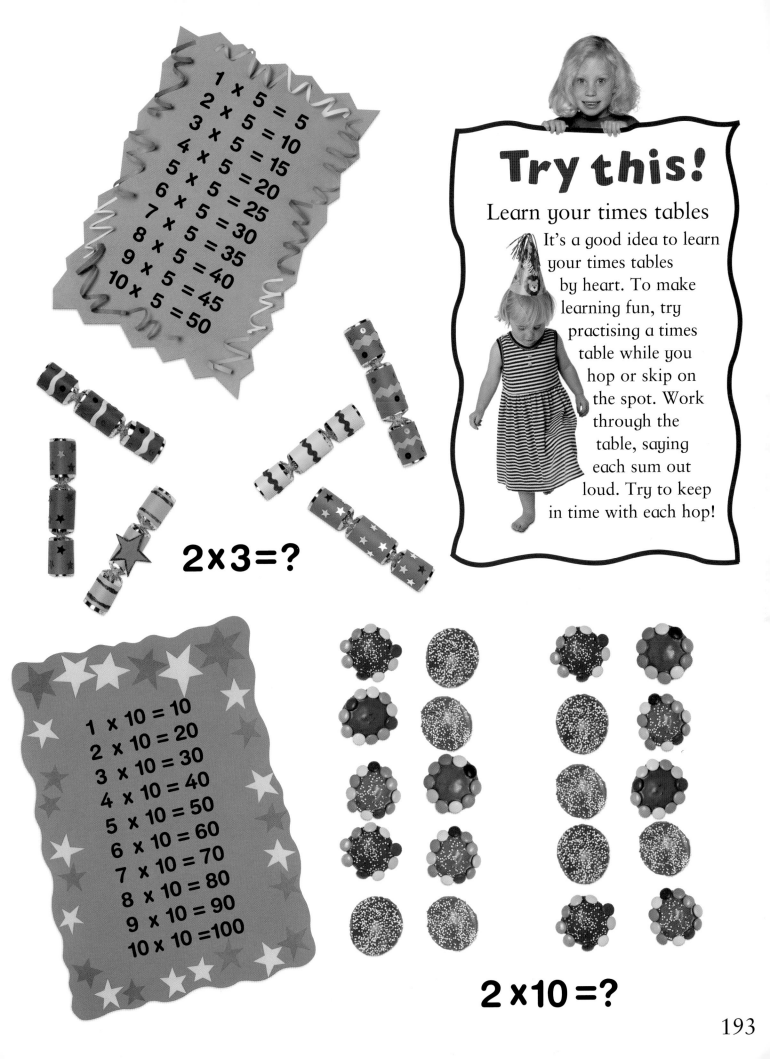

$$1 \times 5 = 5$$
$$2 \times 5 = 10$$
$$3 \times 5 = 15$$
$$4 \times 5 = 20$$
$$5 \times 5 = 25$$
$$6 \times 5 = 30$$
$$7 \times 5 = 35$$
$$8 \times 5 = 40$$
$$9 \times 5 = 45$$
$$10 \times 5 = 50$$

Try this!

Learn your times tables

It's a good idea to learn your times tables by heart. To make learning fun, try practising a times table while you hop or skip on the spot. Work through the table, saying each sum out loud. Try to keep in time with each hop!

$$2 \times 3 = ?$$

$$1 \times 10 = 10$$
$$2 \times 10 = 20$$
$$3 \times 10 = 30$$
$$4 \times 10 = 40$$
$$5 \times 10 = 50$$
$$6 \times 10 = 60$$
$$7 \times 10 = 70$$
$$8 \times 10 = 80$$
$$9 \times 10 = 90$$
$$10 \times 10 = 100$$

$$2 \times 10 = ?$$

Share it out

Two wicked pirate chiefs are sharing out the treasure. How much should each one have?

Pirate Pete

How many hats will Pete and Penny get?

4 maps of buried treasure.

How many different jewels are there? How many will each pirate have?

Share out the flags between the pirate chiefs.

caw-caw!

caw-caw!

Will each pirate get a parrot?

Is there a spade (shovel) for each pirate?

These fierce teddies are the pirate ship crew.

Is there a tankard for both pirates?

Count up the telescopes. How many are there for each pirate?

How will you share out this glittering gold?

Pirate Penny

These 4 treasure chests are overflowing with treasure. Can you split them between Penny and Pete?

10 wooden barrels full of confectionery. Can you share it between the two pirates?

How many teddies does each pirate chief get?

Divide it up

Sometimes you need to share out lots of things. Dividing is a way of making equal groups. Another word for this is sharing.

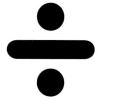

This sign means divide by.

This sign means equals.

This is how you write the sum.

6÷2=3

6 pretty ribbons   2 cows   Each cow has 3 pretty ribbons

This is how you write the sum.

10÷2=5

10 lumps of sugar   2 horses   Each horse has 5 lumps of sugar

This is how you write the sum.

2÷2=1

2 eggs   2 hens   Each hen has 1 egg

Try this!

1. Take a piece of paper and draw 2 farmers, 2 hats, 4 cows and 6 horses.
2. Cut the pictures out.
3. How many hats, cows and horses for each farmer?

Try writing this as three sums, using the ÷ sign.

This is how you write the sum.

20÷5=4

20 sheep   5 sheepdogs   Each sheepdog has 4 sheep

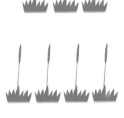
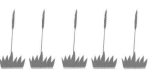

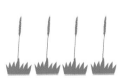

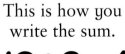
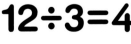
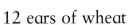

This is how you write the sum.

12÷3=4

12 ears of wheat   3 mice   Each mouse has 4 ears of wheat

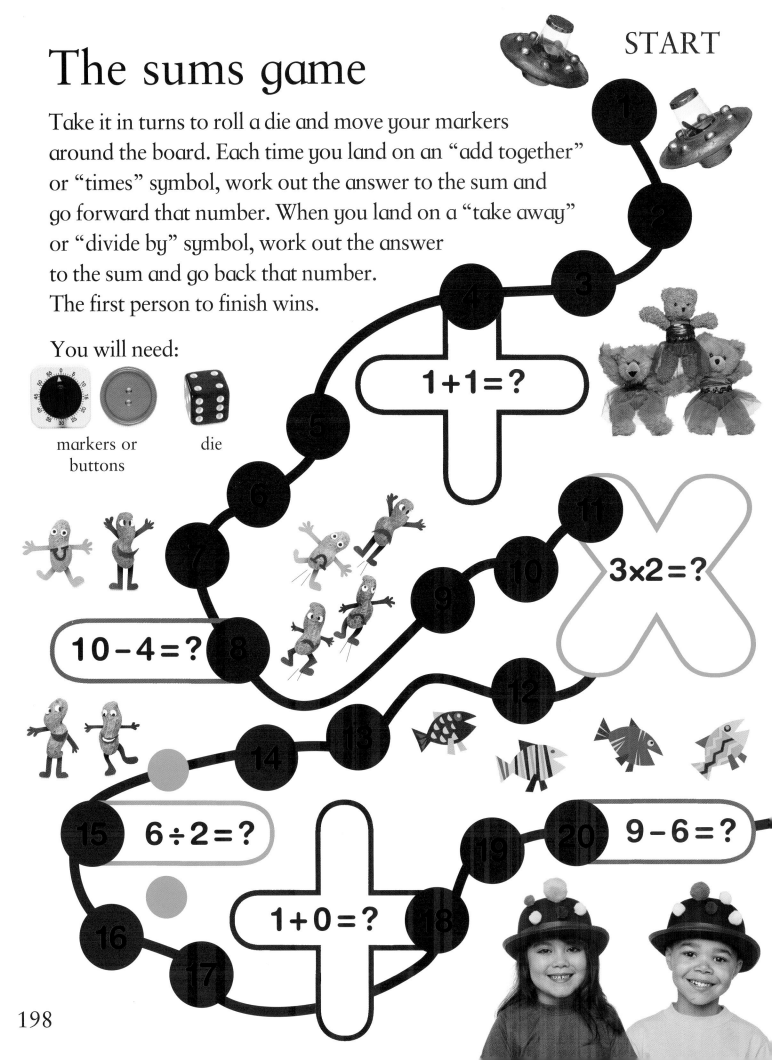

The sums game

Take it in turns to roll a die and move your markers around the board. Each time you land on an "add together" or "times" symbol, work out the answer to the sum and go forward that number. When you land on a "take away" or "divide by" symbol, work out the answer to the sum and go back that number. The first person to finish wins.

You will need:

markers or buttons

die

START

1 + 1 = ?

3×2 = ?

10 – 4 = ?

6 ÷ 2 = ?

1 + 0 = ?

9 – 6 = ?

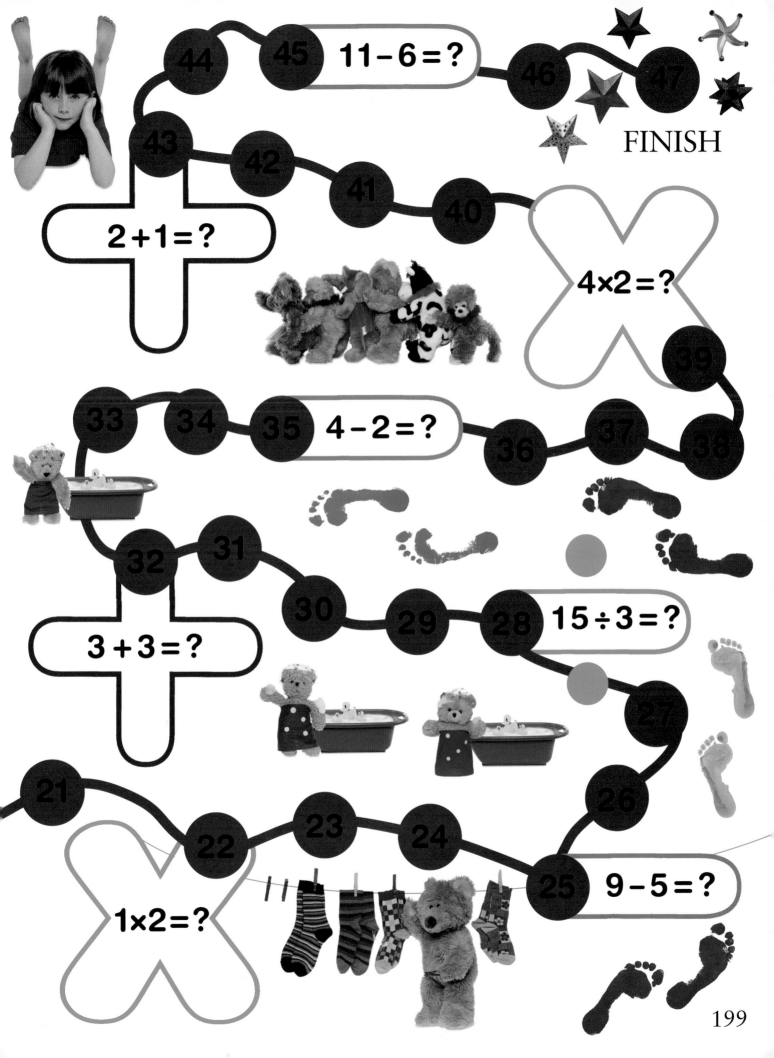

44

45

11 − 6 = ?

46

47

FINISH

43

42

41

40

2 + 1 = ?

4 × 2 = ?

39

33   34   35   4 − 2 = ?   36   37   38

32   31

30   29   28   15 ÷ 3 = ?

3 + 3 = ?

27

21

26

22   23   24

25   9 − 5 = ?

1 × 2 = ?

Try this!

A memory game

1. Place ten things from around your home on a plate.

2. Ask a friend to look at them for one minute. Cover the plate.

3. How many things can your friend remember?

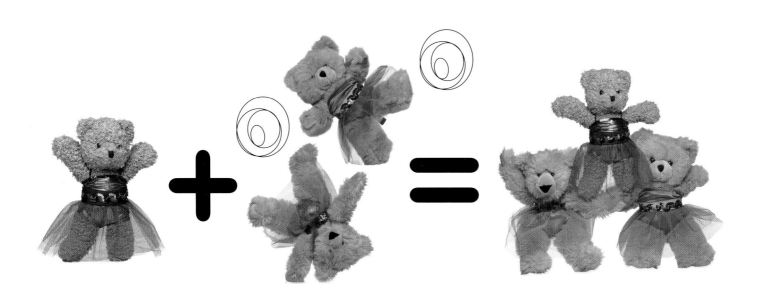

TIME

Day

It is light during the day.
People are busy working
and playing.

Wake up, Teddy,
it is a sunny day!

What do you
do in the
daytime?

When
would
you
wear
these
clothes?

making music

playing dominoes

going for a ride

Night

It is dark at night.
Most people go
to sleep.

Goodnight,
Teddy!

Try this!

Make a waking-sleeping doll

1. Draw a person on a piece of card. Cut it out.

2. On one side, draw a person in pyjamas.

3. On the other side, draw a person in day clothes.

When would you wear these clothes?

Morning, afternoon and evening

Each part of the day
has a different name.

Morning

The first part of
the day is called
the morning.

I eat
breakfast.

My big sister goes to school.

Afternoon

We call the
second part
of the day
the afternoon.

I eat
lunch.

Sometimes
my friends
and I
dress up.

Evening

The last part
of the day is
called the
evening.

We eat our supper.

My sister
reads me
a story.

I get dressed.

I might play some music.

Sometimes I do a puzzle.

My sister comes home from school.

Try this!

Draw your day

On a piece of paper, draw what you did in the...

1. ...morning...

2. ...afternoon...

3. ...and evening.

We go to bed.

How long does it take?

Everything you do takes time. Some things take a short time, other things take longer.

It only takes a short time to make a mess...

It takes a long time to make a cake...

...but only a short time to eat it!

...but it takes a longer time to clear it up.

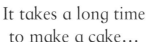

It takes a long time to build a sandcastle...

It takes me a long time to make a tower...

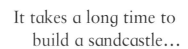

...but only a short time to knock it down.

It takes my sister a long time to eat her supper...

...but the puppies eat theirs in a short time.

Try this!

How long does it take?

Find some sunflower seeds and...

...cress seeds.

Plant the seeds. Remember to water them.

Which grew first?

sunflower   cress

...but only a short time to destroy it.

Days of the week

A week is seven days long. Each day of the week has a different name.

Monday

Tuesday

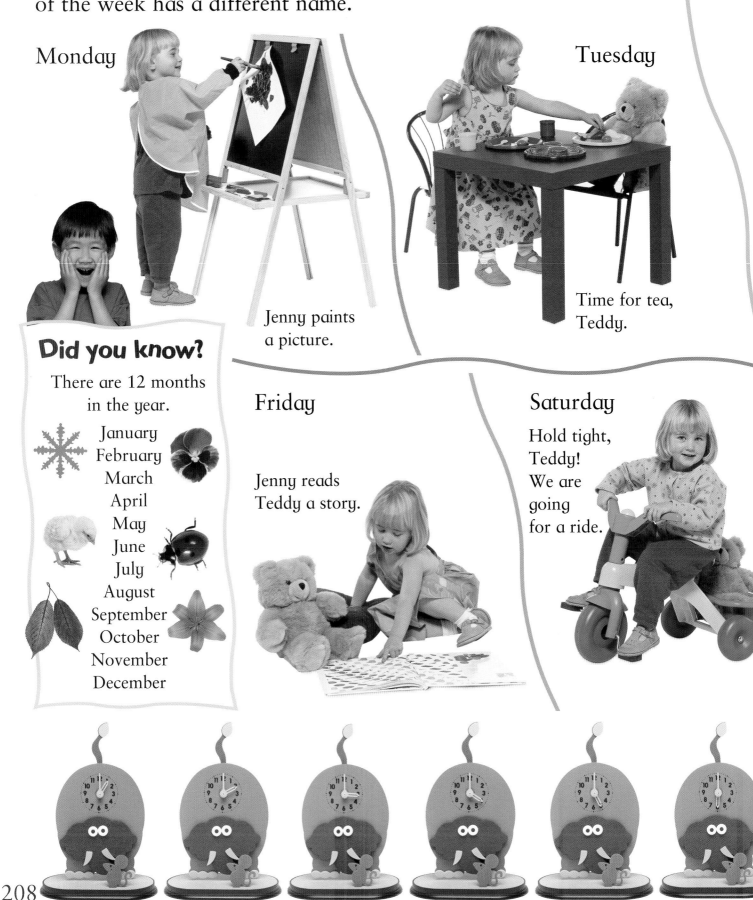

Jenny paints a picture.

Time for tea, Teddy.

Did you know?

There are 12 months in the year.

January
February
March
April
May
June
July
August
September
October
November
December

Friday

Jenny reads Teddy a story.

Saturday

Hold tight, Teddy! We are going for a ride.

Wednesday

Do you like swimming? Jenny and Teddy do.

Thursday

Jenny and Teddy are playing outdoors.

Try this!

Keep a diary for a week

1. In a notebook, divide each page into three sections.

MONDAY	TUESDAY

2. Draw what you did in the morning, afternoon and evening.

MONDAY	TUESDAY

Sunday

Teddy is poorly. Doctor Jenny is looking after him.

3. Colour in your pictures. Draw all your week.

MONDAY	TUESDAY

Tomorrow is Monday again.

209

Clocks and watches

We can tell the time by looking at a clock or a watch. Look at all these different clocks and watches.

Who is sitting on top of this clock?

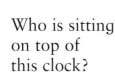

Who uses an alarm clock in your house?

Do you like this sports watch?

A kitchen timer counts down the minutes. A bell rings when it gets to zero.

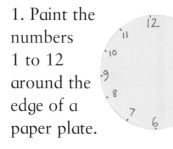

Try this!

Make a clock

1. Paint the numbers 1 to 12 around the edge of a paper plate.

2. Make two hands from card. Attach them with a paper fastener.

You can use a stopwatch to time how long something takes.

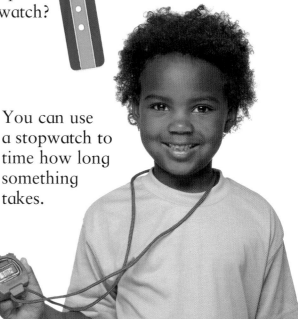

Do you wear a watch?

Most wrist-watches have round faces.

This alarm clock is set to go off just before 7 o'clock.

This is a digital clock. The time is 3 o'clock.

Can you tell the time? This clock says it is 3 o'clock.

A nurse's watch can be pinned on to a uniform. Its numbers are upside down.

Do you know where this famous clock is?

Wobbly birds keep track of time.

Do you have a clock?

On the hour

A day is divided into blocks of time called hours.

The big minute hand takes one hour to travel right round the clockface.

The little hour hand takes one hour to move between two numbers on the clock.

When the big hand is on the 12, we say it is something o'clock.

Dragon Bob has a very busy day today.

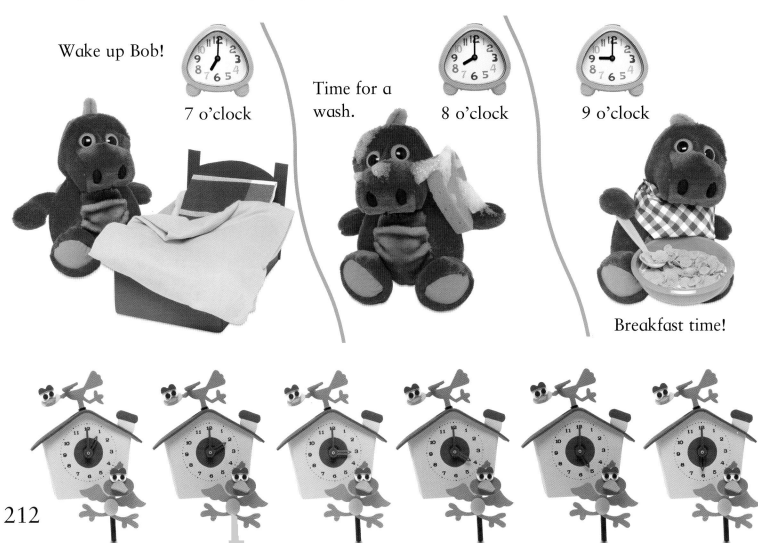

Wake up Bob!

7 o'clock

Time for a wash.

8 o'clock

9 o'clock

Breakfast time!

10 o'clock — Don't forget to brush your teeth.

11 o'clock — Time for a story.

12 o'clock — Lunchtime!

1 o'clock — Who said dragons can't paint?

What pretty flowers! — 2 o'clock

Look at my tall tower. — 3 o'clock

4 o'clock — Supper time!

5 o'clock — Where does this go?

6 o'clock — Time for bed.

213

Half hours

When the hour hand is half way between
two numbers, we say it is half past the hour.

When it is half past, the
big hand is on the six.

When it is half past,
the little hand is
between two numbers.

When
the big
hand is
on the
six, it has
moved
halfway around
the clockface.
We say it is half
past something.

These are all halves.
It takes two of them to make a whole.

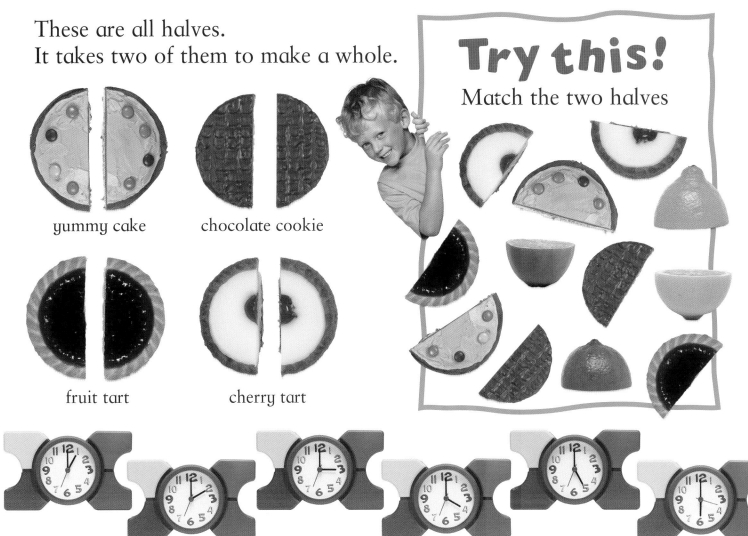

yummy cake

chocolate cookie

fruit tart

cherry tart

Try this!

Match the two halves

214

Welcome to Ted's amazing circus!

Half past twelve Time to get ready.

Half past one  Trick riding.

 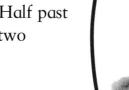 Half past two

Don't wobble!

  Half past three

Cartwheels galore.

 Half past four

It takes two to tumble.

 Half past five

Hey, why is everyone upside down?

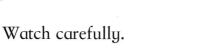

 Half past six

Watch carefully.

  Half past seven

Got you!

Quarter past

When the minute hand is on the three,
we say it is quarter past the hour.

When it is quarter past,
the big hand is
on the three.

When it is quarter past,
the little hand is just
past a number.

When the
big hand
is on the
three, it
has moved
a quarter of
the way around
the clockface.
We say it is quarter
past something.

These are all
quarters. It takes
four of them to
make a whole.

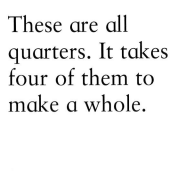

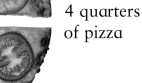

4 quarters
of pizza

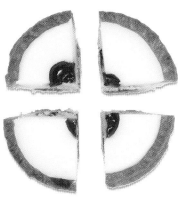

4 quarters of
cherry tart

4 quarters of
chocolate
cookie

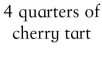

4 quarters of
fruit tart

 **Quarter past twelve**

What shall I do with my hair?

  **Quarter past one**

How about bunches?

 Quarter past two

Do topknots suit me?

 **Quarter past three**

This pony tail looks like a pineapple...

 **Quarter past four**

...and now I look like an octopus!

  **Quarter past five**

Flowers look too cute!

 Quarter past six

Grips are itchy...

  **Quarter past seven**

...but a bow is just right!

217

Quarter to

When the big hand is on the nine, we say that it is quarter to the hour.

When it is quarter to the hour, the big hand is on the nine.

When it is quarter to the hour, the little hand is nearly at a new number.

When the big hand is on the nine, it has moved three-quarters of the way around the clockface. There is only one quarter more to go. We say it is quarter to something.

Try this!

Match the quarters

Ted is doing his exercises.

Quarter to one

Bend and stretch. Touch your toes.

Quarter to two

Skipping is fun.

Quarter to three

Yikes! I hope I can get up again!

Quarter to four

Phew! These weights are heavy.

Quarter to five

A big, big stretch.

Quarter to six

Jogging along.

Quarter to seven

I like hula hooping.

Quarter to eight

Let's finish off with a nice cool swim.

219

What time is it?

Look at all the things that Alien Bill did in one day – he's been very busy! Can you tell the time on each clockface?

What's the time?

Morning exercises.

What's the time?

Baking a cake.

What's the time?

Wrapping a present.

Party games.

What's the time?

What's the time?

Time to go home.

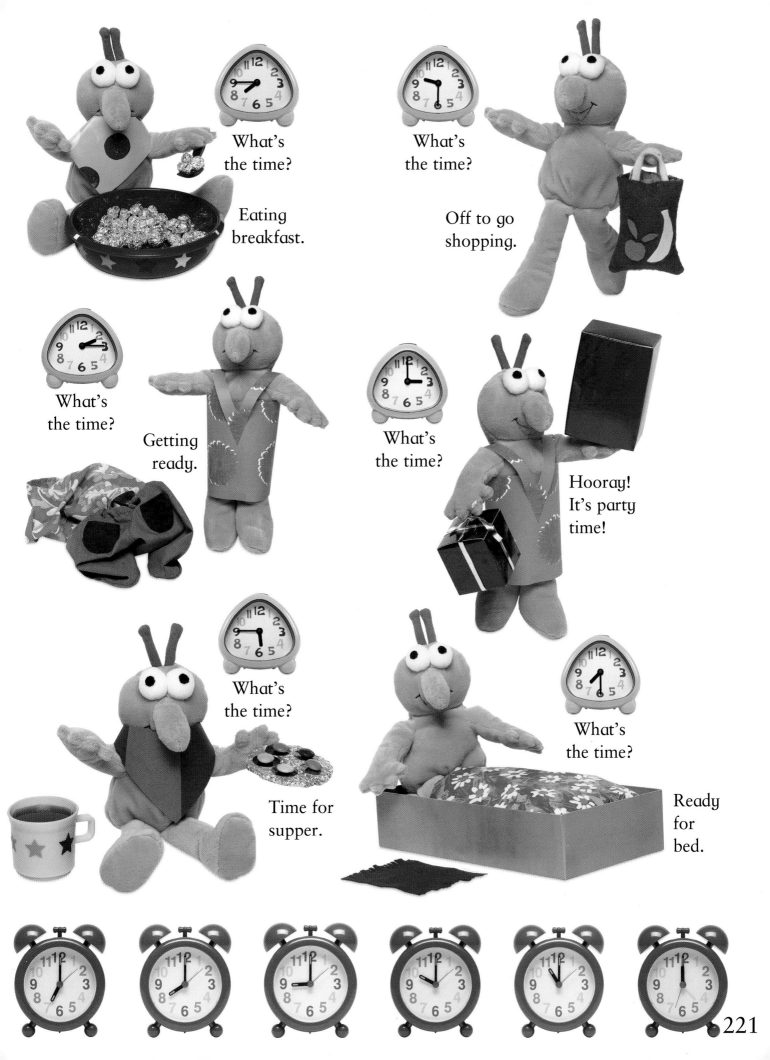

What's the time?

Eating breakfast.

What's the time?

Off to go shopping.

What's the time?

Getting ready.

What's the time?

Hooray! It's party time!

What's the time?

Time for supper.

What's the time?

Ready for bed.

221

Just a minute!

A minute is a short time, but a second is even shorter. There are 60 seconds in one minute.

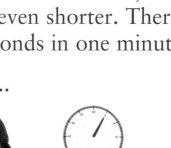

The numbers on a stopwatch go up to 60. It takes one minute for the hand to go all the way round the clockface.

Can you....

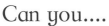

...skip for 5 seconds?

...do a funny dance for 60 seconds?

...do star jumps for 20 seconds?

...jump in a sack for 15 seconds?

...bounce on a bouncing ball for 10 seconds?

…click your fingers for 25 seconds?

…march for 30 seconds?

…jump up and down for 45 seconds?

…catch a ball for 35 seconds?

…clap your hands for 55 seconds?

…balance a pot on your head for 50 seconds?

…hop for 40 seconds?

On time

Sometimes, we have to do things at a certain time.

Nearly
4 o'clock

It is
nearly
time for
supper.

Just after
2 o'clock

**TOYTOWN
2pm**

Oh no!
Teddy is
too late
for his
plane.

Exactly
12 o'clock

It is time
for the teddy
bears' picnic.

Almost
6 o'clock

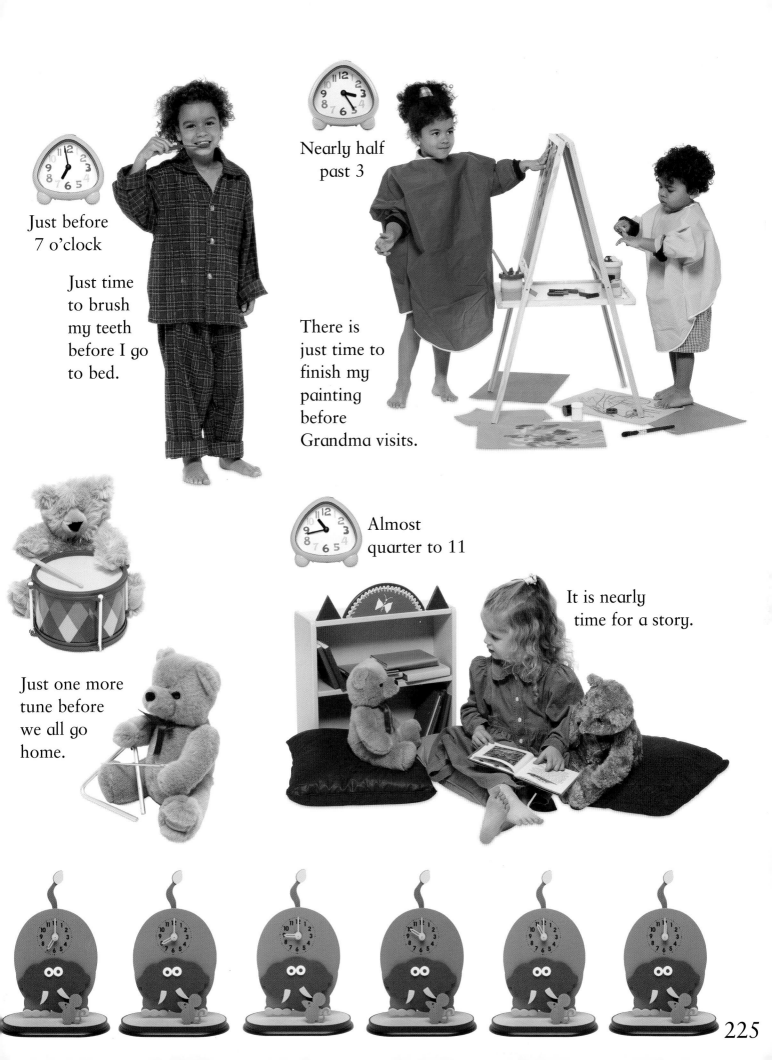

Just before
7 o'clock

Just time
to brush
my teeth
before I go
to bed.

Nearly half
past 3

There is
just time to
finish my
painting
before
Grandma visits.

Almost
quarter to 11

It is nearly
time for a story.

Just one more
tune before
we all go
home.

Match the time and clockface

Read what is happening and then find the clock that shows the same time.

Dragon Bob has supper at five o'clock.

Teddy is skipping at quarter to two.

Holly has a pony tail at half past one.

Alien Bill goes shopping at 2 o'clock.

Alien Bill goes to a party at quarter to four.

It is just after two.

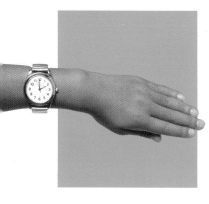

Dragon Bob brushes his teeth at 10 o'clock.

Holly puts grips in her hair at 3 o'clock.

Just before six, I brush my teeth.

Teddy is juggling at half past four.

Alien Bill is baking at quarter to three.

Dragon Bob has a wash at 8 o'clock.

Alien Bill waves goodbye at quarter past six.

Holly puts a bow in her hair at quarter past seven.

Bob goes to bed at 7 o'clock.

Teddy is walking the tightrope at 5 o'clock.

Try this!

Crazy orchestra

Make funny music by blowing bubbles in a glass of drink, banging bowls and wobbling a sheet of card.

SCIENCE

Things that move

Things can move quickly or slowly, forwards or backwards, or even round and round!

Ben and Sam move fast, but Jane is too slow!

Beep!
Beep!
Beep!

I can move forwards ...

... and backwards.

up and down

How do these things move?

around and around

You can move in lots of different ways. Can you make ...

... tiny steps?

... giant steps?

Did you know?

The sleek cheetah is the fastest animal on Earth.

Wheels are round.

Wheels help things move smoothly and easily.

This wheelbarrow is easy to move but ...

... this one isn't. Can you see what's missing?

All these things have wheels.

bicycle

toy tractor

skateboard

The fire engine will move quickly down this slope ...

... but faster down this slope. Do you know why?

Try this!

Make a pull-along cart

1. Trace around a cup to make four wheels. Cut them out.

2. Push two pencils through two wheels. Fix them with modelling clay.

3. Make four holes in a small box. Push pencils into the holes.

4. Fix wheels to the other end of the pencils with modelling clay. Tie string to one end.

Push and pull

When you push or pull, you can make something move.

pushing a go-cart

Pull, Emma ...

Pull hard, Emma and Sam ...

How do you make ...

... a toy dog move?

Pull harder, Emma, Sam and Anna ...

... a scooter move?

Hooray! They've done it.

Try this!

Magic bucket

Pour a little water into a bucket. Swing it round and round, with a straight arm.

The water will be pushed into the bucket, and it won't fall out!

Ted has to push and pull to make the swing move.

Wheee! This is fun!

Push and pull some clay to make a fierce dragon!

When you get dressed, you ...

... pull up your socks

... push your feet into your shoes

... push your hands into your gloves

... pull on a t-shirt

... pull down your hat

Pull your lips and push out your tongue. What a funny face!

233

Floating and sinking

Some things, like boats and ducks, float on water. Other things sink.

Diving Bear will find out which things sink.

Try this!

Make a sailing boat

1. Cut a triangular sail from card. Glue on a straw.

2. Fold the card over the straw. Fix with adhesive tape.

3. Press modelling clay into the base of a tub.

4. Push the straw into the modelling clay.

A sailing boat floats.

Ducks float on water ...

... and so does Ted's rubber inner tube.

... sinking gold coins

... an anchor

Diving Bear finds things that sink ...

... a pirate's sunken treasure chest

... sand, pebbles and shells

Drop lots of different things into some water. Which ones float? Which ones sink? This is called an investigation.

pencils

socks

wooden blocks

Draw what happens on a sheet of paper.

sink float

plastic toy

pebbles

ball

clay

balloon

apple

banana

leaves

flower

feather

Balloons like to float. Push a small balloon ...

... and a big balloon under water.

Which one is easier to push?

235

Air and wind

You can't see air, but it's all around you. There is even air inside your body!

Have you ever ...

... blown bubbles full of air?

The air in this bag came from John's lungs.

... pumped air into a balloon?

... seen bubbles of air in a fizzy drink (soda)?

... blown out birthday candles?

When air moves, it can make other things move. Wind is moving air.

On a windy day ...

... a windsock fills with air

... hair gets blown about

... a kite flies

... leaves flutter

Try this!

Make a whizzing balloon

1. Thread a straw on to a long piece of string.

2. Inflate a long balloon. Stop the air escaping with a clamp.

3. Tape the straw to the balloon.

4. Ask friends to hold the ends of the string. Release the clamp. The balloon will whizz away!

These things have air inside them –

arm floats

soccer ball

balloons

bouncing ball

Pretend to be the wind. Blow on to the sails to make the boats move.

An umbrella can be turned inside-out by the wind.

Gravity

Things fall to the ground because of an invisible force called gravity.

Going up is hard work ...

... but sliding down is easy!

Wheee!

What goes up ... must come down!

When you jump into the air ...

... gravity pulls you down.

A slinky spring slinks down.

These toys work because of gravity.

The marble rolls down the marble run.

Gravity pulls the woodpecker down the stick.

tap

tap

Did you know?

There is no gravity in Space. If you threw a ball, it would float away from you.

What happens if Peter stops juggling?

Orange juice!

Which of these things falls the fastest and reaches the ground first?

A piece of paper or ...

... a ball of paper?

Two identical balls?

A feather or ...

... a plastic toy?

Will the ball roll up or down the slope?

Try this!

Make a gravity painting

1. Mix up runny paints and pour spoonfuls on to card.

2. Tip the card side to side, and backwards and forwards. The paint will run and make patterns.

239

Balance

If something is balanced, it will not topple over.

Roll up and watch Freddy Frog and his friends balance ...

One of these towers will fall over because it is not balanced.

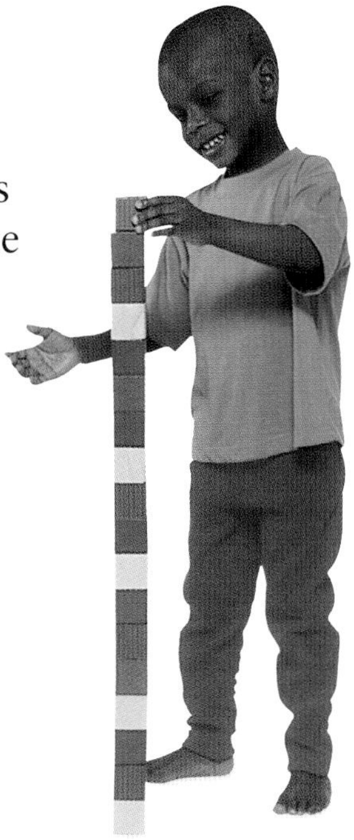

Do you know which one?

... a spinning plate

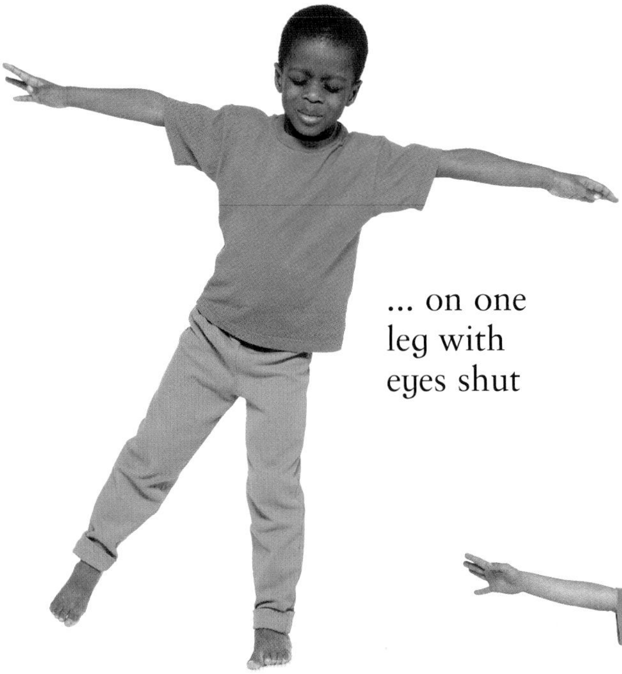

... two cherry cakes

... on one leg with eyes shut

... on a drum

... on stepping stones

... on a tightrope

Try this!

Make a stand-up person

1. Fold a large rectangular piece of card in half.

2. Draw a person on it. The head is near the fold.

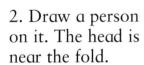

3. Cut it out, but do not cut along the fold.

4. Draw a face. Open the card to make your stand-up person balance.

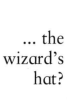

Which of these is balanced?

The ice cream or ...

... the wizard's hat?

This chair ...

... or this wobbly one?

This tower ...

... or this one?

This seesaw ...

... or this seesaw?

Spin around in a large, open space to make yourself dizzy.

When you stop, is it hard to keep your balance?

241

Hot and cold

Hot and cold things feel different to touch. Some things change when they are heated up or cooled down.

To make yourself warm ...

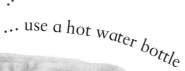

... rub your hands together

... use a hot water bottle

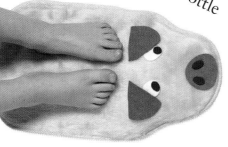

phew!

You sweat when you're hot.

brrr!

You shiver when you're cold.

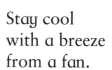

... wrap up well

Stay cool with a breeze from a fan.

Some food has to be kept cold in a refrigerator.

Yuck, warm sour milk!

Try this!

Crunchy chocolate cakes

1. Wash your hands. Break 125g/4¼oz of chocolate into pieces. Ask a grown-up to help you melt it.

2. Mix the melted chocolate with 2 cups of crunchy cereal.

3. Spoon it into paper cases. Place them in the refrigerator to go hard.

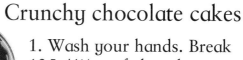

Here are some things that change when heated or cooled. Take care! Hot things can burn you.

Cheese melts ...

... when it is cooked.

Chocolate melts in your warm fingers.

Frozen water is solid.

Melted ice is liquid.

Chocolate cake batter becomes ... cooked cake.

Butter ... melts on hot toast.

Yummy ice cream ...

Cook a raw egg to make ... a scrambled egg ... or a fried egg.

... melts when it gets warm.

Your body

Your body has lots of different parts. You can see some parts, but others are hidden under the skin.

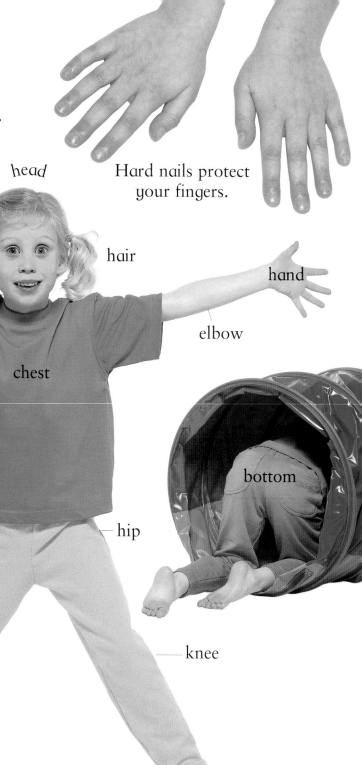

head

Hard nails protect your fingers.

fingers

arm

hair

hand

elbow

chest

Can you feel your hard skull ...

waist

bottom

... and the bones in your knees?

hip

leg

knee

ankle

foot

toes

There are lots of bones in your feet.

The bottom of your ear and the tip of your nose are soft.

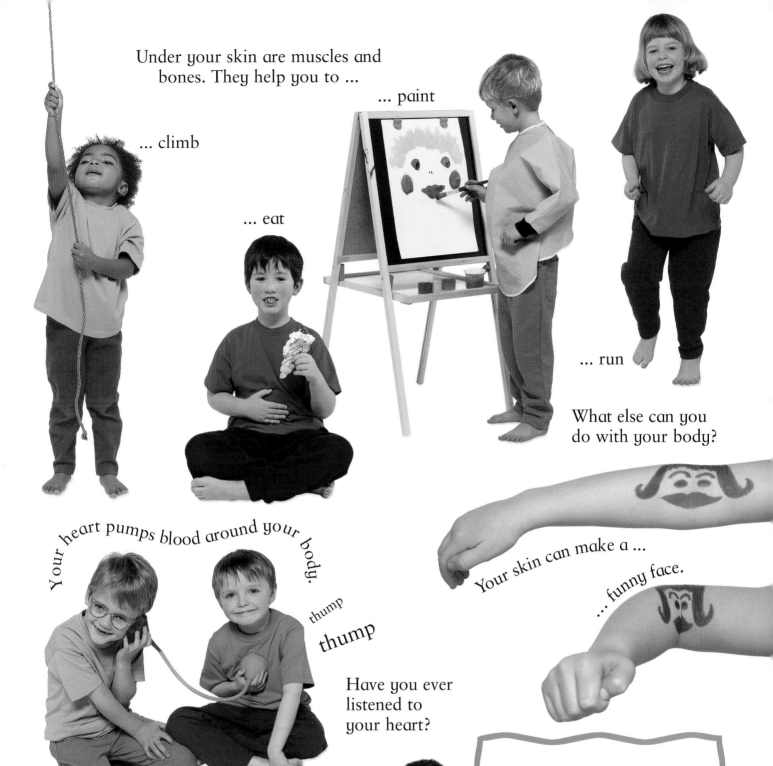

Under your skin are muscles and bones. They help you to ...

... climb

... eat

... paint

... run

What else can you do with your body?

Your skin can make a ...

... funny face.

Your heart pumps blood around your body.

thump thump

Have you ever listened to your heart?

You go to sleep at night because your body needs to rest.

Did you know?

Your brain tells your body what to do. It is inside your head. Your brain weighs about the same as 12 apples.

Growing

All living things grow and get bigger. To grow, they need food, water and sunlight.

big girl

little girl

Look at how much Fred has grown!

baby girl

Fluffy chicks grow up to be chickens.

Puppies grow up to be dogs.

A hairy caterpillar goes to sleep in a cocoon and changes into a butterfly.

When some animals grow, they change completely!

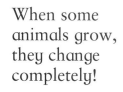

Try this!

Growing a bean seed

1. Get some bean seeds.

2. Push the seeds into some soil.

3. Put in a sunny spot and water each day.

4. Watch your bean seeds grow.

You wouldn't eat soil for dinner, but growing plants get their food from soil.

Look at how a hyacinth plant grows. Where are its roots?

 It starts as a bulb.

 It then grows a leafy stem.

Leaves and a flower bud grow.

Leaves grow taller and the flower opens.

Frogs lay eggs called spawn. Tadpoles hatch from eggs and grow into frogs. Croak!

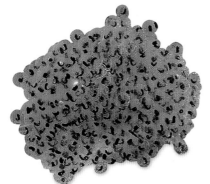

247

Touching and feeling

You feel with your skin. You can learn about things by the way they feel.

strawberry

orange

banana

What do these fruits feel like?

pineapple

mango

grapes

Ouch!

A prickly holly bush.

Your sense of touch warns you of danger.

We like to wear things that feel nice. Which of these things would you wear?

A soft sweater or ...

... a scratchy one?

Fluffy grey slippers or ...

... scrubbing brush slippers?

Try this!

A feely picture

1. Glue felt, foil and abrasive paper on to card.

2. Use cotton wool, sponge, card and shells to make a seaside scene.

248

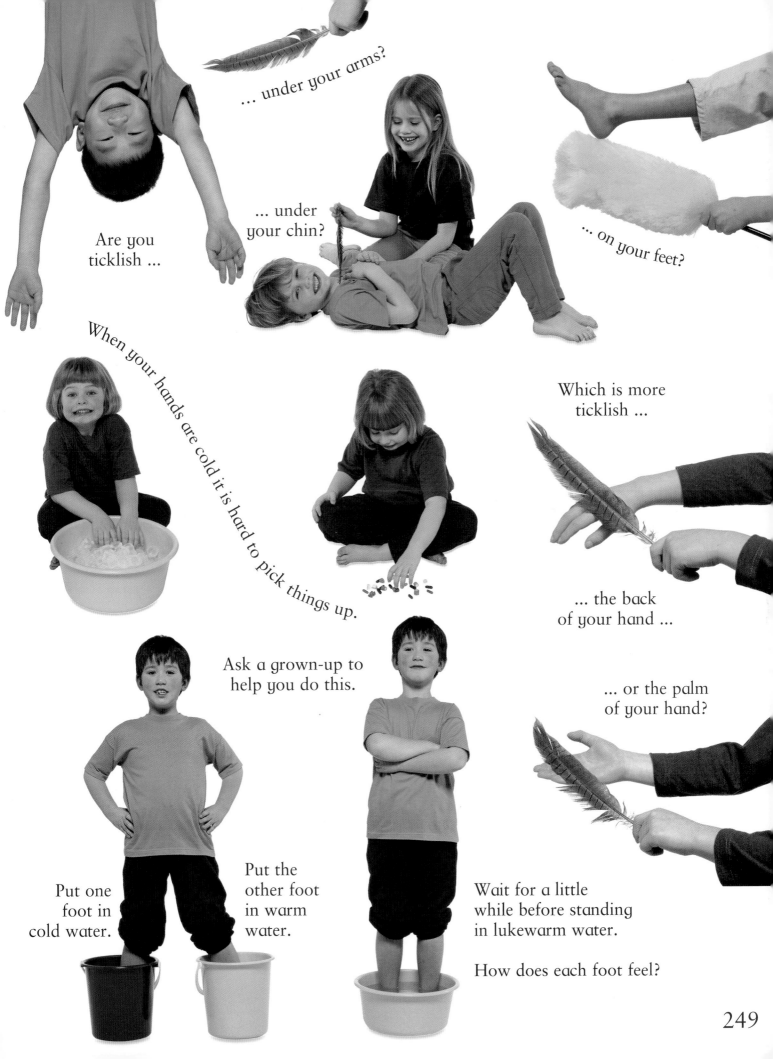

... under your arms?

Are you ticklish ...

... under your chin?

... on your feet?

When your hands are cold it is hard to pick things up.

Which is more ticklish ...

... the back of your hand ...

Ask a grown-up to help you do this.

... or the palm of your hand?

Put one foot in cold water.

Put the other foot in warm water.

Wait for a little while before standing in lukewarm water.

How does each foot feel?

249

Sound and hearing

Our ears help us to hear sounds.
Sounds are made by moving air.

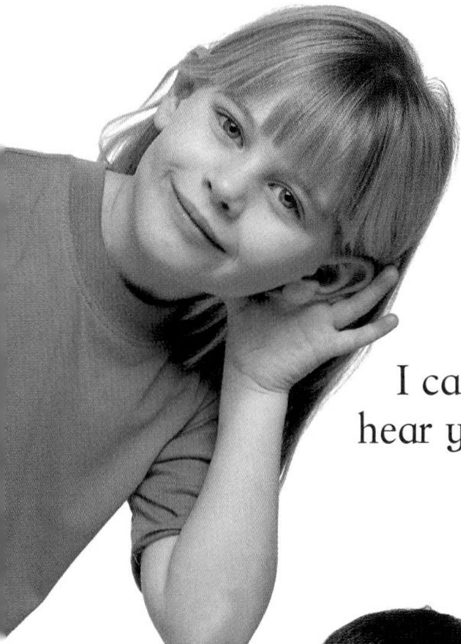

I can
hear you.

I can hear
you too.

What a lot of noise!

brrr
brrr

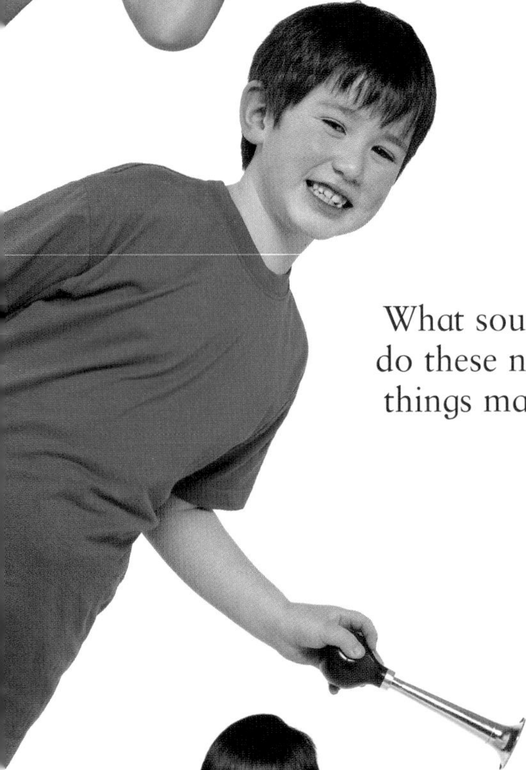

What sounds
do these noisy
things make?

jingle
jingle

honk!
honk!
honk!

bang!
crash!

toot
toot

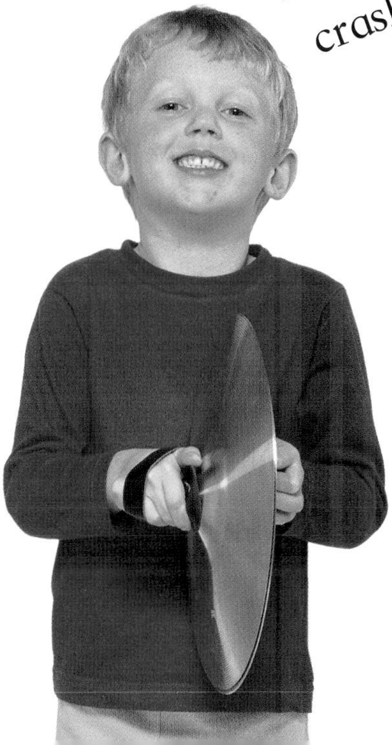

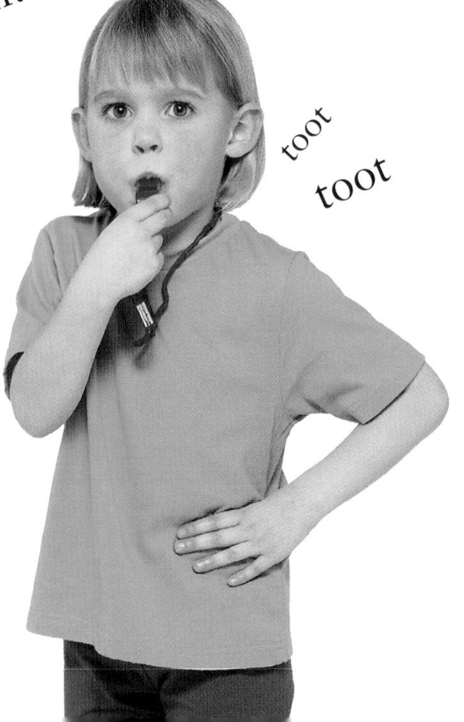

Did you know?

Elephants a have excellent hearing.
They can hear one another from
at least 4km (2½ miles) away.

Try this!

Sshh! A whispering game

1. Sit your friends in a circle. Make up a silly rhyme.

2. Whisper it to the friend sitting next to you.

3. Keep going until the whisper gets back to you. Is your silly rhyme still the same?

Record yourself talking and singing, then play it back.

Does it sound like you?

Your voice will travel through this tube.

Sounds can change. Try shouting into a bucket.

Your tongue helps you make sounds.

Sing with your tongue like this ... and then like this.

Does your voice sound different?

251

Making music

When air is squashed or moved it makes a noise. Different things are used to squash and move air to make music.

clap, clap, clap with my hands

twang twang on my guitar

tap, **tap**, **tap** with my shoes

maracas

thump thump thump on the floor

xylophone

ting ting ting on my triangle

castanets

recorder

drum

la la la with my voice

You can make music using things in your home. You can make ...

... a loud sound

... low sounds

...or high sounds

... a quiet sound

... windy sounds

... lots of different tinkling sounds

... soft rustling noises

... very loud noises

Try this!

Make a shaker

1. Get some dried lentils or beans.

2. Put them in a plastic cup.

3. Place a cup on top. Join them with tape.

4. Shake it up and down and side to side to make sounds.

Question and answer game

Answer the questions and then make your way through the wiggly maze to see if your answers are correct. Give yourself a point for every question you get right.

What happens if the popsicle gets warm?

John goes down the slide.

It melts.

What does a puppy grow into?

A dog.

What happens next?

What happens when Sam blows on the candles?

The candles will go out.

254

What do red and yellow make?

Orange.

It falls down.

They make a loud noise.

What happens to the wobbly tower?

What happens to the apple?

What can a seed grow into?

What happens when Tom bangs the cymbals?

It falls down. Crash!

A plant.

Hooray, you've made it! How many points did you get?

FINISH

255

Try this!

Talking with your fingers

Use your fingers to spell out the word "talk" instead of saying it. This is called sign language. It is used by some children who are deaf or who are unable to talk with their voices.

t   a   l   k

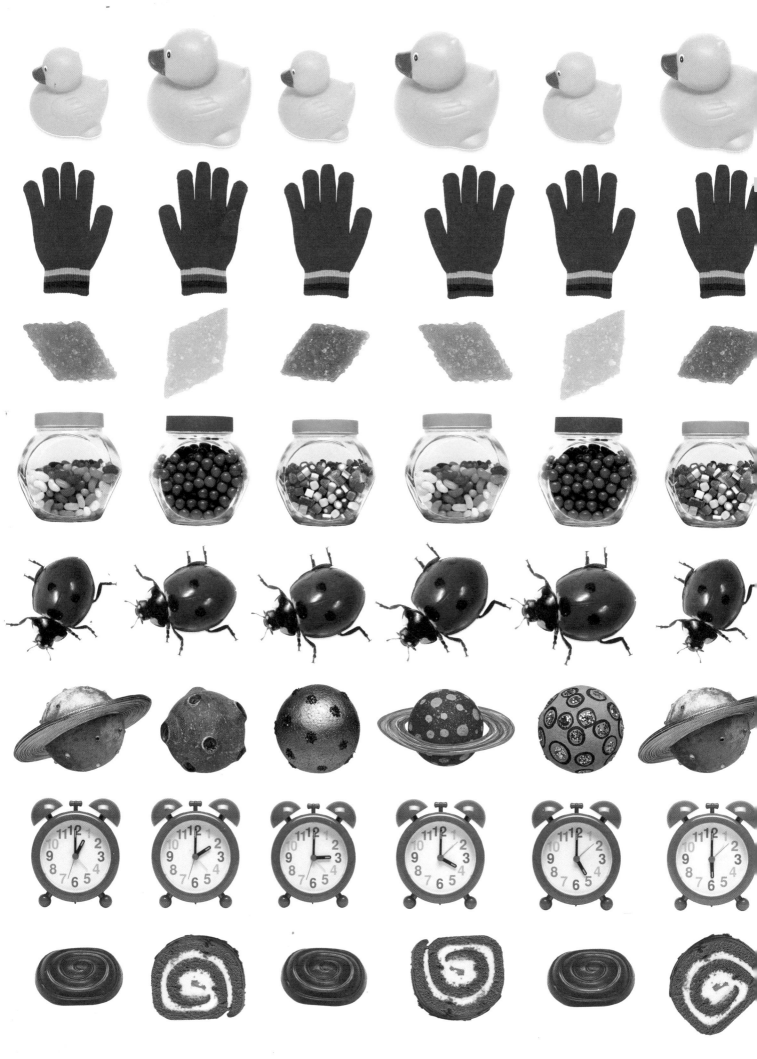